'HOW TO'

BOOK OF
BASIC
GARDENING

ANN BONAR

BROCKHAMPTON PRESS

The **'HOW TO'** Book of Basic Gardening explains in straightforward terms – through the use of concise texts, charts, photographs, and diagrams; the principles and techniques that will enable you to gain more enjoyment from your garden.

'HOW TO'

Contents

The 'How To' Book of Basic Gardening
was conceived, edited and designed by
Simon Jennings and Company Limited

This edition published 1996 by
Brockhampton Press Ltd,
20 Bloomsbury Street,
London WC1B 3QA

Text and illustrations
© 1981 Simon Jennings & Co Ltd

ISBN 1 86019 204 1

Printed and bound in U.A.E.

THE AUTHOR

Ann Bonar is usually
described as a
horticultural journalist –
a label which tends to
obscure the facts that
she is both an
experienced
horticulturist and a
successful writer. She
has many years
experience of
commercial fruit
growing, and has
regularly contributed to
a number of journals on
gardening topics. Her
other titles in this series
are: *Vegetable
Gardening*, *Herbs and
Herb Gardening* and
Flower Gardening.

Introduction

Most of us have a space outside our homes and most of us attempt to keep it tidy, if not easy to look at. Whether it consists of bare soil, or whether it is covered with paving, bricks or concrete, a variety of plants will be growing on it. If left completely untouched, most of these plants will be weeds, tangled, living and dying, and not particularly ornamental.

With only a little help, this space can still have a variety of plants growing in it, but it can be a chosen variety – colourful, fragrant and healthy. Going a step further, it can provide food: potatoes, lettuces and tomatoes, strawberries, apples, or melons – and flavourings: parsley, mint, garlic.

However, a good many home owners, faced with this space, perhaps for the first time in their lives, either decide that growing plants on purpose needs too much technical knowledge, or that it is going to take more time and work than they can supply.

Nothing could be further from the truth. There is a great deal of unnecessary fuss made about cultivating plants, i.e. gardening, so that it is surrounded with an aura of green-fingers and double-digging

But if you remember that plants are alive, as you are, and need food and drink and air, as you do, you are halfway to being a successful and enthusiastic gardener. One way in which plants 'eat' is by absorbing particles of minerals – potassium, sulphur, iron – dissolved in water through their roots.

Another way in which they obtain the fuel they need to go on living is by making other foods, and oxygen, out of the air with the help of the energy provided by the sun. Much of your gardening is aimed at providing the best possible conditions for both these activites.

Basic Gardening will show you, in words and pictures, how to do the essential work needed in running a garden easily and efficiently. Simplicity will be the key-note – after all, gardening is only a matter of sticking a plant in the ground and watching it grow. The mystique which has grown up round that fundamental action has developed because human curiosity led to experiment, and finally resulted in the complicated scientific art which modern gardening can, but need not, be.

5

What is a garden?

A garden can be exactly what you want it to be; the only essential is that it must have plants in it. However, the gardens for every day in temperate climates will have in them somewhere, a patch of lawn, mainly to act as an outdoor 'carpet', flowering shrubs, some trees for shade, herbaceous plants to provide colour and flowers for cutting, and an area for growing food.

But a garden can be so much more than a haphazard collection of plants and features. Put together without thought, the result is a jumble. A meadow of wild flowers left to its own devices is more satisfying to look at. However, with forethought and a little imagination, it can look as though it just 'growed' – as nature intended.

There are no limits to the variety you can achieve. You can collect rare plants, you can go in for undercover cultivation – greenhouses, cold, cool or warm – exotic plants and tropical fruits. You can become a botanist or a herbalist, grow flowers for painting or photography, or experiment with breeding new plants. The possibilities in the garden are endless – but remember to keep some plants in it somewhere so that it can be called a garden.

The formal garden
This perspective view of Denham Place, Buckinghamshire, possibly painted by John Drapestier *c.*1700 is a fine example of the English formal garden of the period. At the time, French influence dominated garden design and required that the house be at the centre of an axial plan in which perspective is the critical factor.

The elements of gardening

Once you have decided that the weed-infested wilderness outside the sitting-room window needs to be tamed, if only for the sake of the neighbours, you will save yourself energy, time, frustration and cost if you first find out a little bit about what is involved in dealing with plants.

To start with, bare soil will be covered in plants sooner or later. If you clear the weeds off that wilderness and leave it bare, more will grow in their place. If you dig it and leave it for a few weeks with a fence round it, weed-seeds in the soil will be stimulated by digging into germinating.

So you will do better to choose what you want to grow, order the seeds or

plants, and have them ready to put in as soon as the ground is cleared. In other words, all through your gardening life, replace a weed with a plant you want, as soon as you can.

You will need to know the basic techniques of dealing with the soil – digging, hoeing, raking, watering – so that plants can get the food and moisture they want from it. You will need to know the right way to sow and plant, and when to cut off new growth and when to leave it alone.

An essential part of gardening successfully is an awareness of the weather. The start and rate of plant growth is greatly dependent on the weather – warmth, lots of sunlight and plenty of moisture will make plants grow very fast. Cold dry, dull weather will produce a standstill.

You can get to know what kind of weather is likely in your district at various times of the year. You can also learn by observance all through the year which parts of the garden are sunny or shady, and which parts are frosty, wet or windy.

Observation is an important part of gardening, particularly if you want to grow healthy plants. It must be close observation, too, of minute changes in a plant's appearance. In this respect, looking at other people's gardens and plants is important, especially the national gardens and national shows. If you are a beginner, you will need to have some criteria for what is good growth, good cropping, or good colour in a given plant.

It is extremely important to work with the plants, that is, to supply them what they need when they need it. Seedlings and young plants in particular should be thinned, transplanted, pricked out, watered and fed, at exactly the right stage – the leeway is only a few days. Too soon, and it will be a waste of time; too late and the plant will always be weak; either way the plant will be damaged.

It helps if you know something about the way a plant works as well. Its internal mechanisms are nearly as complicated as ours. Because it is not obviously mobile, it is not necessarily inactive. Far from it: the internal tissue of a plant is a seething mass of activity. Apart from anything else, it has to adjust itself constantly to deal with rain, frost, hail, drought, wind, heat, diseases and pests – and your own operations on it.

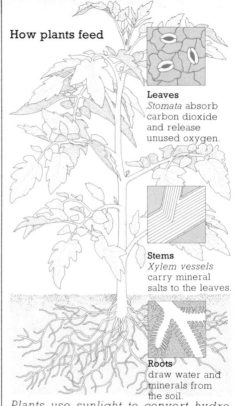

How plants feed

Leaves
Stomata absorb carbon dioxide and release unused oxygen.

Stems
Xylem vessels carry mineral salts to the leaves.

Roots
draw water and minerals from the soil.

Plants use sunlight to convert hydrogen, derived from water drawn up by the roots, and carbon dioxide into sugar compounds which it uses as food. This is part of the process called photosynthesis.

9

The site

If you have taken over an established garden, already planted, but perhaps uncultivated for some months, it will have a variety of good plants in it that are worth keeping. There will of course be some that you do not like, or that are weak and diseased.

But before you start cutting down or digging up wholesale, make a plan of the garden on paper, go round the garden and mark on it the plants that seem to be worth keeping; mark them, too, with a stick, and then start work. Dig carefully, in summer there may be dormant bulbs, or in winter perennials, which have retreated underground.

Making a plan
Before starting work, make a plan of your garden and the plants you want to keep. Use the planner on page 93 to help your design.

Suiting the site
Walls, *left*, can create ideal conditions for a great variety of plants. The climbing wistaria, *top*, the saponaria, *centre*, and the delicate agapanthus, *bottom*, are popular examples. Water, *top right*, suits irises and primulas but Rodgersia and alchemilla, *bottom*, prefer moist shady conditions. Dry, exposed sites can be difficult but they suit lavender, *below*.

Utilizing the site

Walls and fences – the vertical space – are parts of a garden often neglected as places for decorative plant growth. However, they are often ideal for providing a background for climbers and twiners to scramble up, and all but the north-facing aspects provide warmth, so that tender peaches, grapes, passionflowers or jasmine can grow safely.

Don't be discouraged by what might appear to be impossible conditions in your garden. Suppose you have sandy or shingly soil on a sloping site which gets the sun all day – certainly you could not grow foxgloves, violets or marsh marigolds, the shade and water lovers, but you could try the Mediterranean plants, such as rock and sun roses, lavender, thyme and rosemary. Similarly, if you have a very wet patch of ground, instead of draining it, leave it as it is and put in plants that grow naturally in marshy soil, or close to streams or pools. If you find that chalk predominates in the soil don't try to grow rhododendrons and azaleas, even in special pockets of the acid soil they like. They will never flower really well. Try instead syringa, lilac or forsythia; the results will be large, healthy, heavily flowering shrubs.

Shade, wind, salt air, sandy or peaty soil – whatever the characteristic of your garden, there will certainly be something that will grow well if you work with the site, rather than force it to grow plants unnatural to it.

If you have an awkwardly shaped garden, for instance a corner site, or a long and narrow one, making the most of it will be a matter of concentrating on design rather than the plants. You can do a great deal to disguise its fundamental shape with internal hedges, terraces, gardens within the garden and twisting paths.

A small garden can be made to appear much larger by the judicious use of hedges, which can in themselves be a major feature. A flat, exposed site can be made interesting with quickly growing shrubs and trees, which will give privacy as well.

The climate and weather

In countries which have a cycle of the four seasons, spring, summer, autumn and winter, plants have geared their growth to the regular rise and fall of temperature that occurs from spring to winter, and to the equally regular increase and decrease in the length of the days.

On the whole, the change in temperature has the most effect, other factors being equal. Warmth, allied to the presence of moisture and nutrient, produces quick elongation of shoots and leaf production, and hastens the maturity of the plant, which is one method of ensuring the continuance of that species.

Cold slows plant growth to such an extent that it can stop altogether and the plant exist in a state of suspended animation, for weeks, months or even years, until warmth returns.

In temperate climates, there is usually more than enough rain to supply the moisture the plant needs, but in late winter and in spring, there is often not intense enough light to guarantee good growth.

In your own garden, there will be variations on the general trend of the climate, brought about by the geography of the surrounding countryside, and by the presence of buildings, woods or fields. By experience and with the help of diaries, you can get to know what these changes will be.

In particular, learn to be your own forecaster; transplanting followed by rain will be much more successful than doing it in hot and brilliant sunshine.

Microclimates

While your garden will follow the general pattern of climate in your area, within it conditions can vary considerably from site to site. Because cold air is heavier than hot, it tends to collect at the lowest part of the garden. If there is a barrier to its free downward flow, such as a fence or a hedge, it collects and concentrates – producing a frost pocket, which can extend upwards considerably depending on the degree of cold.

A site which faces south and is protected from the north and east by a wall or a screen of plants or trees, will always be much warmer than the rest of the garden. Some parts of the garden which are always in shade will never be as warm as the rest of the garden. You should allow for this difference when choosing plants.

Planning your garden

There is one point of view that says the best gardens just grow of their own accord. A 'planned' garden can certainly look awkward and out of context, and the best planning is the kind which isn't obvious – careful thought beforehand which acts as an unseen guide to the choice and arrangement of plants. The most natural arrangements will often look completely unplanned, but it may well have taken years of careful work to achieve this effect. Equally, a garden which is intended to have a more formal appearance cannot be constructed overnight, yet the final design has to be conceived before work is started.

Natural or formal

Whatever kind of garden you intend to have, it is wise to work out a basic plan before you start work. Even the apparently unplanned garden, *right and bottom right*, could only be created with careful forethought – gardens left to their own devices would not look like these. Even a very simple arrangement using annuals around a stepping stone path, *above left*, requires some prior consideration if it is to look good. Vegetables, *bottom left*, can look very attractive in a carefully arranged and balanced plot. Small, fairly formal gardens, *below*, look best if they are made to a preconceived design.

Planning considerations

Your very first considerations must be the soil and the aspect. Both can be altered and modified to some extent, but their basic nature will largely prevail. The garden exposed to wind will require suitably tough plants, or shelter: fences, hedges, walls or screens. Gardens in a frost pocket will forbid the presence of tropical plants, unless you are prepared to buy a greenhouse and heat it.

The kind of soil is most important, too. You will first need to decide

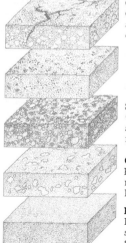

Clay soil
Greyish soil, heavy and sticky when wet; cracks when dry.

Sandy soil
Gritty to the touch; drains quickly and is loose in dry weather.

Shingly soil
Contains many small stones or gravel; makes poor topsoil.

Chalk soil
Pale and often shallow; may contain flints and lumps of chalk.

Peat soil
Dark brown, flaky and springy. Fertile but tends to be acid.

whether it is acid or alkaline, with the help of a soil-testing kit. Some plants grow very well on acid-reacting soil, others won't grow at all. Remember that it can vary from one part of the garden to another.

Then you should determine what kind of soil it is, whether it is fundamentally clay: heavy and sticky to feel when wet, cracking severely when dry – sandy: gritty to the touch, nearly always dry and not waterlogged after heavy rain – shingly: stony or gravelly – chalky: usually pale coloured with lumps of chalk – peaty: dark brown to black, spongy, and very acid in reaction, or possibly none of these, but the ideal loam.

The needs of yourself and your family come next; do you want plants to provide food? Are there children, and if so what sort of play areas do they need? Is the garden basically for recreation, a room outdoors, or is it a major hobby? How much time have you to spare for it? How much money? Do you own pets? Are you thinking of keeping hens, rabbits, bees?

If it is a brand new garden, then you start with a clean sheet. If you have taken over one already established, have a careful look at what is already there. Some plants you will be able to keep; others will be a waste of space. If you can wait a little before making major changes, you will discover how well the garden's lay-out fits your needs – paths are often in the wrong places. You will also find out how temperature and light vary from one part of the garden to another, and from one time of the year to another.

Basis of choice

Growing your own food is more than likely to be one priority: do you want to concentrate on vegetables or fruit, or grow some of each? They can be the everyday kind, like potatoes, cabbages and plums; luxury crops which are expensive to buy – asparagus, peaches – or vegetables for the gap in supplies in late winter and spring. Don't forget the family's personal preferences, either.

Somewhere to relax and entertain, and somewhere for the children to play will necessitate an outdoor carpet or a stretch of green of some kind. Alternatively a patio, paved, bricked, or similarly surfaced, and perhaps a sandpit, make alternatives for very small gardens, or ways of cutting down labour. If you have a child with green fingers, a border to itself will be very popular.

You should also decide whether you are a plantsman or an artist. The former will collect and grow, higgledy-piggledy, all kinds of plants, for various reasons; the latter will choose plants according to their colour and shape. You can try both, but nearly always the individuality of the garden is lost. If you are a plantsman, do you want to specialise? Alpine plants, roses, herbs, greenhouse cultivation, plant breeding, dahlias – these are just some of the possibilities.

Cost is not now a negligible factor in choosing plants and designs. Some plants are very expensive indeed. Going in for bedding arrangements may provide instant gardens, but you will have to pay for it. Plants ordered from nurseries will have carriage and packing costs added.

Gardening is an absorbing hobby, but it takes time. How much have you got to spare, and at what times of the year? Do you want to spend most of your non-earning hours in the garden, or do you want easy-care plants?

Ornamental variety
Flowers can create as many effects as there are gardens. Whether it be the brilliance of massed colour, *top left*, or a concentrated seasonal effect like that of tulips in a spring garden, *right*. In awkward situations needing low-growing plants, the mesembryanthemum, *below*, is perfect for making a carpet of colour. Damp and shady gardens, which often include a large number of foliage plants, are ideal for hostas, *bottom left*. They produce lilac or white trumpet-shaped flowers in July.

The flower garden

The ornamental garden in which plants are grown mainly for their flowers will contain herbaceous kinds with soft tissues, rather than the hard tissues of bark and wood. They include border perennials, bulbs, annuals and so on, most of which are relatively small. So the smaller gardens will consist largely of this class of plant. Hence the size of your garden will have a bearing on the type of ornamental you grow.

Herbaceous plants rely on their flower colour for most of their attraction; blending or contrasting shades, tones and tints will be most important. Seeing the plants in flower at nurseries and national gardens will help in your choice.

Shrubs and climbers

The traditional herbaceous border shows them off well; island beds in grass are attractive, too, but less formal, and prevent the garden looking too stiff. Annuals or bedding plants in clumps provide brilliant massed colour. Biennials and spring-flowering bulbs will be a tonic after the drabness of winter.

Flowers for cutting come largely from herbaceous plants; a bed discreetly set aside specially for these, not too far from the house, will avoid spoiling the garden display.

Herbaceous plants grow best with warmth and shelter from wind: hedges, walls, or fences are essential. There are some beautiful but tender plants, such as agapanthus and schizostylis, which can be grown in the garden with south-facing vertical faces.

The pool and the rock-garden are aspects of the flower garden whose special needs require them to be carefully sited; make use of the natural hollows or humps if possible.

No garden can afford to be without shrubs. They are the best plants for ensuring privacy and providing a dense cover of leaves and shoots from ground level up to $4\frac{1}{2}$m(15ft) and as much in width. They also create shelter, and careful choice and planting can create sun-traps in the garden where the more fragile plants can be grown.

It is the shrubby plant which is used for hedges and screens; this is the commonest form when shelter and privacy are wanted. But a group, or groups, of shrubs will do the same job without the regular and frequent formal clipping that hedges demand.

Once planted and established, they do not need much care besides pruning and, even so, there are only a few that require annual treatment. Troubles are few. They can cover large areas of ground, so that you do not have to spend a lot of time dealing with that area, or they can be tiny shrublets, growing in an herbaceous border. But, unlike the perennials, they will need hardly any attention.

Shrubs are the main source of colour in the garden during the winter, because many are evergreen, and some of these have leaves patterned in yellow, cream or white, or purple. You will find, too, that some flower in winter.

The climbing shrub does a particularly good job of screening, hiding blank house walls, the sides of sheds and garages, and mundane necessities like dustbin shelters and oil storage tanks. Roses, clematis, wisteria and honeysuckle are amongst the most attractive of any garden plant; between them they can maintain flowers, fragrance and leaves all the year.

The reaction of the soil is important in deciding on a selection of shrubs. Practically all those belonging to the plant family which contains the heathers – rhododendrons, azaleas, heathers, pieris and so on – must have acid-reacting soil, preferably with good drainage. But even if you have an alkaline soil, you still have about four-fifths of the shrubs available from which to choose.

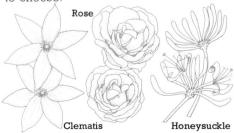

Rose

Clematis   Honeysuckle

Lawns and trees

Your decision on whether you want a lawn at all depends partly on whether you need an area for recreation, and on whether you have the time to mow it; during spring and summer it will need cutting every week. You can overcome the mowing problem to some extent by having an Alpine lawn, that is, grass mixed with native flowering plants, allowed to grow between the cuttings to a height of 10 or 12cm (4 or 5in).

But if you want somewhere to play games – rounders, tennis, croquet – it will need a good deal of time and labour to keep it in good condition.

Grass will grow on most soils, provided they are not extremely acid or alkaline, but although it will grow in shade in Nature, it does not do so well when cut for a lawn. Even the shade grasses die out gradually.

There is a variety of mixtures of grass seeds, geared to a particular purpose. Bowling-green mixtures produce the finest and most velvety turf; a fine lawn mixture will give a thick close sward; one containing rye-grass will survive a lot of wear and tear. Specialist seedsmen will list a range of mixtures or make up one for your own requirements.

Grass and foliage

There are alternatives to grass, such as creeping thyme, chamomile and clover, but for various reasons, they are best restricted to small areas, out of the way corners, and moderately used paths. They have the advantage of not needing much attention and only occasional cutting.

Your lawn can be grown from seed or turf. Seed takes longer to grow but has the advantage that you choose a mixture exactly right for the site. It costs considerably less than turf, which is said to be seven times more expensive.

Turf will provide 'instant' lawn, but that is about its only advantage, and laying it is heavy work. Moreover, the soil of the turves is foreign to the site and may never amalgamate well.

A garden without trees lacks life and interest. Their vertical growth brings a third dimension to the garden and provides shade and shelter. They are a source of organic matter: leafmould, and of food: nuts, fruit – as well as ornament. Like shrubs, they can be grouped, or grown as single specimens. They will also provide good cover and nesting sites for birds and other wild life, thus enriching the life of the garden and its owners.

Turf and alternatives

The featureless conventional lawn, typified by David Hockney in his painting 'A Lawn Sprinkler', *right*, can be more relaxed if combined with trees. The maples, *bottom right*, need plenty of space but trees are effective in small gardens, as the crab apple, *below*, demonstrates. Those who want something different, might try a thyme 'lawn', *bottom left*. The more usual turf lawn, of course, requires considerable maintenance. The first lawn mower, *top left*, appeared in 1832 and soon became the most essential item in the creation of perfect lawns.

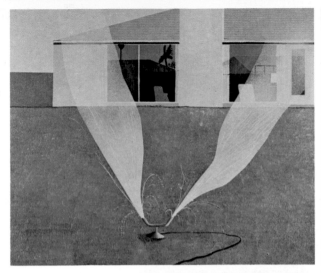

Trees, even when young, are expensive and need careful planting and preparation of soil. Choice of site must be careful too: the mature height and spread must be taken into account and the shade likely to be cast. Tree roots extend considerably sideways, and absorb a great deal of plantfood and soil moisture; the total extent is not definitely known, but can be as much sideways as the height of the tree.

Choice of tree near buildings depends on the soil; if it is clay, the roots of poplars or willows could, but not necessarily, cause trouble with foundations and drains. The small trees and fibrous-rooted kinds, like many conifers, are quite suitable.

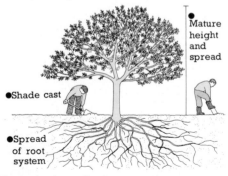

●Shade cast

●Spread of root system

●Mature height and spread

Tree planting – the first considerations

Productive gardens

Most gardens do not have a great deal of room for what were once regarded as necessary but dull plants, so it is important to make the most of the space there is.

Trained forms of fruit trees whose growth is restricted will make the best use of the ground. Apples and pears grown as diagonal cordons and espaliers will be decorative and fruitful, as well as providing shelter and marking boundaries. Fan-trained peaches, plums, gages and Morello cherries will make use of shed or boundary walls; so will dessert grapes.

Blackberries, loganberries and raspberries can take the place of hedges or fences; redcurrants and gooseberries can be grown as upright cordons, and blackcurrants can be trained as fans.

Since all will need protection from birds, they are most conveniently grown on one piece of ground, together with strawberries. A south-facing sunny site is preferable, with the tallest fruits, blackcurrants and loganberries at the back, but blackberries and loganberries will grow in some shade, and facing north.

Before you start planting, make quite

sure you know what the ultimate height and spread of the adult plants will be. Many crops of fruit are much lower than they should be because the bushes or trees have been planted too close. Also, determine the average yield of fruit from a given bush or area – adding to a planned planting 2 or 3 years later can be very difficult.

Vegetables also do best in sunny, sheltered conditions, though a few will grow in shade, and some need shade in summer if they are not to run to flower and seed. To prevent pest and disease build-up in the soil, you will need to practise rotation. Vegetables can be divided into three sections of the garden: the cabbage family, the peas, beans and some of the leafy crops, and thirdly potatoes, fruiting vegetables (aubergine, sweetcorn, etc.) and the rest of the leafy crops.

Use frames for the tender vegetables and some fruit – peppers, tomatoes, strawberries and melons; get them earlier and heavier cropping, and put the frames in the warmest and most sheltered place. Put herbs in a sunny place, not too far from the kitchen. Make sure that an adequate supply of water is always near at hand.

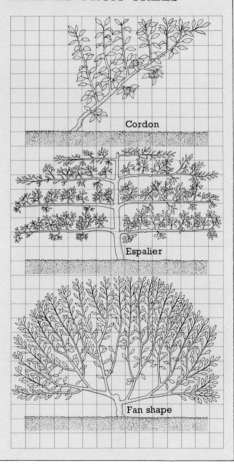

TRAINED FRUIT TREES

Cordon

Espalier

Fan shape

The productive garden

A well-planned vegetable garden, based on crop rotation principles and with a south-facing wall and greenhouse. Ease of access to all plots is provided by hard paths and adequate space is allowed for compost making and storage.

Many other possibilities of planning are available to the vegetable gardener. But remember that most vegetables like sunny, sheltered positions, although some, such as lettuces, will need shade in summer.

The labour saving garden

The best work-free gardens will consist mainly of evergreen, ground-cover plants, shrubs and trees, and lawns, preferably the Alpine kind. Ground-cover plants are trailing kinds, such as ivy, or plants which increase by runners and plantlets – creeping bugle or London Pride – or those with creeping roots or stems. A low-growing cover of this kind will keep out weeds and needs no attention except keeping within the space available.

Protection
Few gardens have any natural protection against birds and frost – so be sure that you have arranged your garden so that you can cloche or net the vulnerable plants.

Easy colour
An arrangement of annuals in and around a patio will provide colour without extreme effort.

LABOUR-SAVING IDEAS

Shrubs are another, larger, form of ground-cover, only needing occasional pruning or cutting back, and trees will supply ornament and shelter with even less attention. Although lawns need mowing frequently, you can get away with that and nothing else, except watering in drought, and still have an area of green.

Plants grown from seed, and bedding plants are out, but perennials and bulbs need little attention. Choose perennials that do not need staking. Shrub roses need little work but modern bush roses (floribundas, hybrid teas) and climbers would not be included. Other climbing plants can be grown, with occasional cutting every few years.

Beds and borders should be reduced to a minimum; especially those in lawns, to avoid work on edges. The soil in them should either be mulched to avoid weeding and watering, or planted to ground-covers.

Paths should be paved, and treated with weedkiller once a season; informal hedges will reduce the need for trimming to a minimum; mowers and rotavators will cut down on grass cuttings and cultivation time.

Choosing a greenhouse

Choice of greenhouse is considerable. The standard is the barn-shaped, wooden-framed, span-roof kind with half walls of brick and swing doors. Nowadays there are also metal-framed houses, glazed to ground-level, with sliding doors; 3/4 span lean-tos, and ordinary lean-tos, for house or other walls, usually with brick half walls; houses made of Dutch lights glazed to ground-level and wooden-framed; home extensions of glass or rigid clear corrugated polythene; plastic walk-in tunnels, or models made of heavy-duty polythene which slip over a metal frame of the conventional barn shape, supplied in a do-it-yourself kit. These are cheap, and stand up very well to strong winds; there is no glass to break but their life is comparatively short. Finally, there are the hexagonal greenhouses (which are more or less circular), wooden-framed, or dome-shaped with multi-angled glass panels and a metal frame.

Ultimately, your choice may depend not so much on what you intend to grow in your greenhouse, but on the initial cost, running costs and the characteristics of the available site.

Span roof
This is the most common type of greenhouse – and has the widest range of uses. They can be glazed to ground level on one side or both.

Lean-to
Lean-to greenhouses may be very cost-effective if they can be placed against a south facing wall of a house. They should then be able to benefit from the heating systems of the house.

Circular and hexagonal
These types are useful for getting maximum light – especially in small or awkwardly shaped gardens. However, they lose heat faster than other types.

Three-quarter span
These greenhouses are gradually going out of fashion – although they can be very useful for fruit trees and vines.

SITING A GREENHOUSE

Ideally, the site for a greenhouse should be well out of the way of shade from buildings or trees. It should be sheltered from wind, especially from the north or east, and be positioned so that it runs north and south. The exception to this is a lean-to, which should face south. A source of water nearby is invaluable, and also access to electricity. Closeness to the home is advisable if it is to be heated, so that keeping up the temperature in winter does not become too much of a chore.

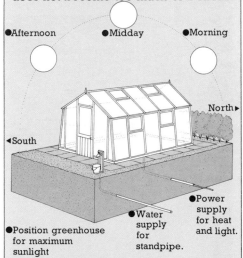

●Afternoon ●Midday ●Morning

North▶

◀South

●Power supply for heat and light.

●Water supply for standpipe.

●Position greenhouse for maximum sunlight

Under-glass growing

Owning a greenhouse opens the door to growing all sorts of tender and tropical plants, fruits and vegetables; even frames and cloches will make all the difference between life and death for some plants, as well as helping to bring plants on early or keep them in flower for longer.

All too often, greenhouses remain empty for a good deal of the year, once the initial enthusiasm has worn off. This is probably because the possibilities for greenhouse plants are not fully realised, and because care of greenhouse plants and management of the greenhouse is time-consuming. A greenhouse is not part of a labour-saving garden.

The plants will need daily attention of some kind; without it they very soon become unhealthy and infested with pests and disease. The greenhouse itself needs regular upkeep, as does the equipment; hygiene is important.

The possibilities
The tropical forest effect, *left*,
may not appeal to gardeners so
much as the usual greenhouse
arrangement, *top left*, but both
views show what can be
achieved under glass, even in a
northern climate.

Range of choice

For satisfying, and controlled, cultivation of tropical foliage plants, *top right*, a heated greenhouse or conservatory is needed. This picture was taken in November in a location where even the daytime temperature of an unheated greenhouse would be too low for many of these plants. The small greenhouse, *bottom right*, is equipped with a heated propagator – so it would be possible to raise plants without heating the greenhouse. Tomatoes, *below*, can be grown successfully, in the greenhouse border.

The greenhouse

When considering what to grow, you will get the most interest for comparatively little cost if you run a cool greenhouse, that is, one with a minimum winter temperature of 7°C(45°F). One or two paraffin heaters can be used, or one of the modern gas heaters. Electric bars or fan-heaters are convenient but expensive; none of these methods requires much work.

With this kind of winter temperature (mainly at night – daytime will nearly always be higher) you can have flowers in the greenhouse in winter. Freesias, primulas, cinerarias and calceolarias are a few possibilities. Others are spring-flowering bulbs and the smaller shrubs potted and brought on early; late flowering chrysanthemums will continue until the end of early winter.

In late winter and spring you can use

it for bringing on seedlings of half-hardy annuals and bedding plants, for starting off tender vegetables early, and for melons or squashes.

In summer its best use is for crops which need a good deal of warmth: tomatoes, aubergines, sweet peppers, grapes, melons – all those fruits and vegetables which in outdoor temperate gardens crop reluctantly, late and poorly. You can grow tropical flowering plants, of course: passion-flowers, bougainvillea, gloriosa climbing lilies and many others, but the outdoor garden has plenty of flowers in summer.

In autumn, tender plants can come in for shelter, quick-growing crops such as radish and lettuce can be sown, and others forced and blanched – chicory, endive, rhubarb. Winter-flowering house-plants which have spent the summer outdoors can come in and be brought on for Christmas flowering; lettuces for next spring can be sown to grow in the greenhouse border – the possibilites are endless.

With a little planning and reading, you can make the greenhouse pay for itself many times over in terms of money and recreation.

Managing a greenhouse

Ventilation of a greenhouse is of great importance, and is the key to healthy plant growth in a greenhouse. Fresh air is essential, and the use of ventilators also regulates the temperature, especially important in summer.

For every 1.8–2.4m (6–9ft) length of greenhouse there should be at least one top (roof) ventilator, and one at the side low down, preferably more. On windy days, ventilators should be opened on the side away from the prevailing wind. In winter, one (or more) at the top should be open just a crack, unless severely cold.

Ventilators can be hand-operated, electrically or chemically operated; the latter are not expensive.

The atmosphere should never be stuffy, or unduly humid (except for special plants, such as cucumbers). However, draughts should be avoided.

With correct ventilation, humidity will also be at the right level without being excessive; meters for measuring humidity are available. In hot dry weather, humidity should be maintained by damping-down the greenhouse two or three times a day, the last time by mid-afternoon.

Maximum light is essential in winter, spring and autumn. The glazing should kept clean and free of leaves and other debris. In summer, shading will be necessary, with washes or blinds. In winter, plastic sheet used as double glazing will unavoidably reduce the available light, but there is now an anti-condensation sheet available.

Very high temperatures are not suitable; most plants are happy with a range between 7° and 33°C (45° and 90°F), depending on whether they are temperate or sub-tropical plants. In winter, various forms of heating can be used: oil, electricity, solid fuel or gas. A maximum and minimum thermometer will be very useful, particularly for recording minimum night temperatures.

Hygiene and cleanliness are vital. The inside of the greenhouse: staging, floor, if concrete or paved, and equipment should be cleaned with a sterilizing solution once a year. Fallen vegetation should be removed, badly diseased or pest ridden plants destroyed, and the house kept free from piles of dirty pots, seed-trays, labels, canes, crocks and other clutter. Try to keep the maximum amount of space available for growing plants.

Propagators

A heated propagator is of great help to the gardener and, if one is available, it is possible to do without heat in the greenhouse. Warmed propagators can be used for germinating seeds, rooting cuttings, starting bulbs and tubers, bringing on tender plants, and forcing strawberries.

A modern propagator will consist of a container, such as a wooden or plastic seed-tray or box, with a clear plastic domed cover, to keep in warmth and humidity. The simplest form of heating is a metal plate warmed by electricity, on which the containers are placed.

There are also propagators which are heated by electric air – or soil – warming cables, an electric light bulb, or paraffin. A thermostat will stop the temperature rising to baking point on warm sunny days.

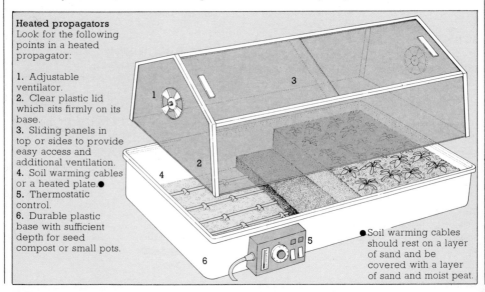

Heated propagators
Look for the following points in a heated propagator:

1. Adjustable ventilator.
2. Clear plastic lid which sits firmly on its base.
3. Sliding panels in top or sides to provide easy access and additional ventilation.
4. Soil warming cables or a heated plate.●
5. Thermostatic control.
6. Durable plastic base with sufficient depth for seed compost or small pots.

●Soil warming cables should rest on a layer of sand and be covered with a layer of sand and moist peat.

Cloches and tunnels

Cloches are a kind of miniature portable greenhouse. Properly used, they can be of great help in increasing and improving edible crops, and in helping to grow ornamentals, especially the tender ones.

Although small, their mobility gives them an advantage over frames and, with a carefully planned programme, they can be in use over successive crops all year round.

They can be used to mature crops early, to keep plants cropping longer in autumn and for ripening sub-tropical crops such as melons, grapes, vines, peppers and so on. For taller crops they can be used standing on end, two round a plant.

Soil can be dried and warmed before sowing outdoors by putting them over the seed-bed some weeks beforehand. Cloched strawberries will ripen at least three weeks earlier than uncloched ones.

Slightly tender herbaceous plants can be protected through winter: sweet peas, gladioli, bedding plants and half-hardy annuals can be planted early and cloched, and so on.

There are many types of cloches: the Chase barn cloche was one of the first, and there are now wire-reinforced glass cloches, opaque white or clear plastic cloches, and plastic sheet tunnels on wire hoops. Cloches can be barn-shaped, round, flat-topped or triangular.

As with greenhouses, the glazing should be kept clean, unless shading is applied in summer.

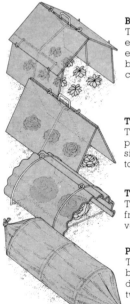

Barn cloche
These cloches are easily moved and very efficient, but glass can be a serious hazard to children.

Tent cloche
These can be glass or plastic and are very similar in application to the barn type.

Tunnel cloche
These cloches, made from rigid plastic, are versatile and cheap.

Polythene tunnel
The cheapest of all, but the polythene deteriorates in one or two seasons.

Garden frames

A frame consits of a low box with wooden, brick, or glass sides, higher at the back than at the front, square or rectangular. It will be 75–120cm × 120–150cm($2\frac{1}{2}$–4ft × 4–5ft), and 14–45cm (6–18in) high, covered with a lid glazed with glass or rigid plastic, and framed with wood or metal. The lid is called a 'light'.

The oldest frames are the English frames, 120 × 120cm(4 × 4ft) the light of which is divided into 15cm(6in) panes of glass set in a wooden frame, usually on a brick base.

The Dutch light, adopted from the commercial growers in Holland, has a wooden frame surrounding a single sheet of glass 75 × 150cm($2\frac{1}{2}$ × 5ft), put on a wooden base.

Frames should be in a sheltered place, protected from north and east, and facing south. Brick or concrete sides will retain most warmth. Closeness to the greenhouse will make watering and moving plants easier.

Use frames for container-grown plants and seeds which need extra warmth, or protection from frost before planting in the open. This is 'hardening-off' and is done by opening the light more and more each day, then leaving

it off altogether during the day, and finally, leaving it off at night.

They are also used for direct planting of tender plants and crops, or direct rootings of cuttings; for plunging pots to ripen bulbs in summer, and for protecting roots of container-grown plants in winter.

Above: A span-roof frame on a brick base and with sliding, or hinged panels.

Below: A wooden frame based on the English light. This one has side wall heating.

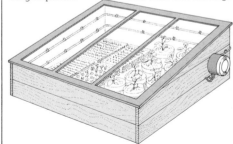

Tools and equipment

To keep the garden in good condition you will need the following tools and equipment: digging fork, spade, metal rake, draw or Dutch hoe, hand fork, dibber, knife, yard broom, shears, barrow, string, sprayer and watering can.

You will also find the following useful in due course: besom broom, secateurs, trowel, cultivator hoe, a garden line, surveyor's tape measure, 6mm and 3mm($\frac{1}{4}$in and $\frac{1}{8}$in) sieves, edging shears, edging tool, a pickaxe, bushman's and pruning saws, step or pruning ladders, long-handled loppers and hose.

The watering-can should be galvanized metal, with a long spout and 2 sizes of rose; the barrow should be metal, with the weight over the wheel.

Secateurs can be rolcut or parrot bill, but for prolonged use the former are more comfortable. Spades, forks etc., can have D, T or Y-shaped handles but the D or Y-shape is the least wearing.

Cutting tools should always be kept sharp and all tools should be cleaned after use and oiled in winter. Sprayers used for pesticides or weedkillers should be meticulously cleaned after use.

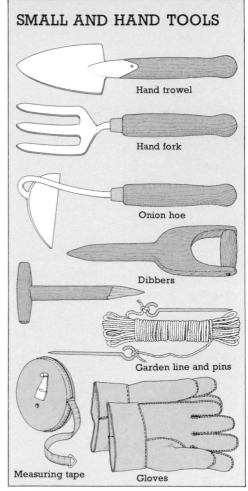

SMALL AND HAND TOOLS

Hand trowel

Hand fork

Onion hoe

Dibbers

Garden line and pins

Measuring tape

Gloves

Hand tools (*overleaf*)
The collection of small tools shown on page 37 includes a hand fork for lifting and trowel for transplanting work. The onion hoe is very useful for weeding under foliage.

Spades
For heavy digging, trenching and ridging, spades are essential.

Forks
Chiefly for lifting, breaking up soil and spreading, forks can sometimes be used in place of spades.

Hoes
There is a wide variety of available hoes, the mosf versatile being the Dutch and the draw hoes.

Rakes
Rakes are necessary for producing a fine crumbly surface and clearing unwanted matter.

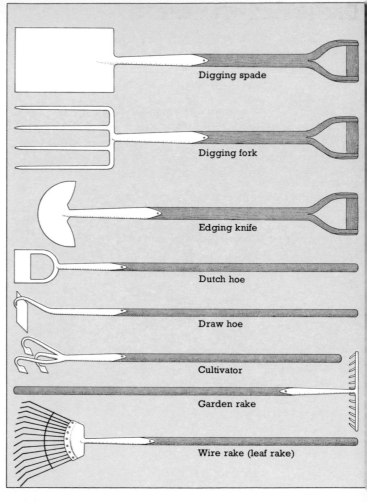

Digging spade

Digging fork

Edging knife

Dutch hoe

Draw hoe

Cultivator

Garden rake

Wire rake (leaf rake)

Gardening equipment

Other equipment
Picks and mattocks may sometimes be necessary for breaking very hard ground. A sieve is a must for preparing seed beds. Wheelbarrows and watering devices are also vital.

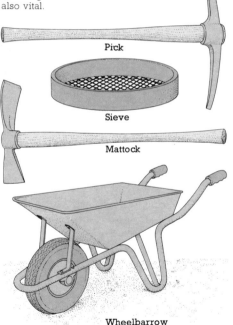

Pick

Sieve

Mattock

Wheelbarrow

WATERING EQUIPMENT

Hose

Sprinkler

Galvanised watering can

Knapsack sprayer

39

Digging

All digging is properly done with a spade, the blade of which is, on average, about 25cm(10in) long. This is the length referred to when digging 'one spit deep' is recommended.

Digging is done to get air into the soil, to get the lower layers weathered, to help excess rain drain through and to mix in plant foods and materials to improve the structure, mostly rotted organic matter such as manure or garden compost.

It is done some months before planting, to allow the turned-over soil to weather, and to allow the additions to be absorbed.

Many plants and most soils will give satisfactory results if 'single-dug'. This means digging a trench to the depth of one spade's length. The soil from the trench is removed to the other end of the site, and another trench is dug next to the first one, the soil from it being used to fill the first.

Organic matter should be mixed with this soil as it is returned, either putting it in the bottom of the trench and then mixing it, spreading it on top of the soil before digging, or forking it in from a barrow as the work proceeds.

SINGLE DIGGING

1. Dig a trench about 60cm (2ft) wide and one spit deep. Remove the soil to the other end of the plot – it will be used to fill the final trench.

2. Dig a second trench alongside the first one, turning the soil into the first trench. Mix in compost or manure as you go. Continue in this way until the end of the plot.

1 spit

DOUBLE DIGGING

Double digging, also called trenching, involves forking and manuring at double the depth of single digging. First and second spit soil must be returned to its own level.

1. Dig a trench one spit deep and 90cm (3ft) wide. Remove the soil to the other end of the plot and use it to fill the final trench.

2. Dividing the trench in half lengthways, dig out the first half another spit deep. You now have a trench with a stepped bottom.

3. Fork and manure the bottom of the deeper trench.

4. Return the second spit to its own depth.

5. Dig a new trench 45cm (18in) wide and one spit deep. Use the soil to fill the first trench to surface level.

6. Continue in this way across the last trench with the soil taken from the first.

1. First trench

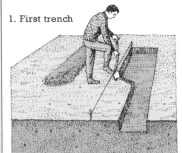

2. Second spit depth

3. Fork and manure

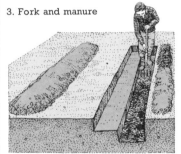

4. Return second spit soil

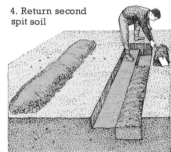

5. Dig new trench

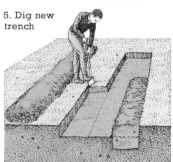

6. Completing the plot

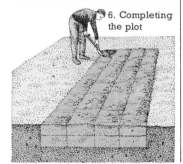

41

Forking

Forking can take the place of single-digging if the soil is in good condition. There should be four prongs, or tines, at least 27cm(11in) long, and the forking will do the most good if done to their full length.

Forking to a few inches depth can be done when working-in lime, and it can be done in the same way when preparing the soil for shallow-rooting vegetable catch crops, or when soil needs turning over before planting, the initial preparation having been done.

Forking is required in half-trenching. This is the same technique as single-digging, but the bottom of the trench is forked a few inches or more deep. Heavy soils and deep-rooting plants will need deeper forking. Organic matter is mixed in to this level at the same time. As with digging, use the tines vertically, so that they penetrate to their full depth.

Forks are the best implements for lifting plants without damaging the roots, and for aerating lawns. When performing the latter operation, press the fork well into the turf but avoid any twisting or turning of the fork as you withdraw it – the object is to get air into the lawn, not to dig it up.

USING THE FORK

◄**Deep forking**
Use the fork vertically so that the tines penetrate the soil fully. Do this when planting deep rooting plants.

◄**Shallow forking**
Fork to a depth of a few inches when applying lime or fertilizers or preparing for shallow rooting vegetables.

◄**Lifting and spreading**
The fork is essential for moving and mixing manures and rotted organic material.

Hoeing

The main object of hoeing is to break up the surface soil and cut through weeds growing in it, particularly the seedling and shallow-rooted weeds. It also breaks up the pan which can occur on the soil surface, that is, the smooth, hard crust that forms with time, or when dry after heavy rain. Thus air circulation and water drainage are improved.

The Dutch hoe is used by pushing keeping the blade almost flat. The user walks backwards, pushing the hoe repeatedly as he goes. The draw-hoe is set at right-angles to the handle, and the hoe drawn towards the user with a chopping action, while the user walks forward. The onion-hoe is similar but very short, 60cm(2ft) or so long, also with a swan-neck.

The Canterbury hoe is like a draw-hoe, but with 3 prongs; the modern cultivator-hoe has 5 tines arranged 3 and 2. Both hoes are also drawn through the soil.

Hoeing is an unavoidable activity in any garden, and one which occurs with great frequency, so it is essential to have soundly made durable implements. Wooden shafted varieties, unless of the more expensive kind, tend to break under stress.

DRAW HOE AND DUTCH HOE

Making a v-shaped drill

◄ **The Draw Hoe**
For breaking up lumpy soil and making drills for sowing, the draw hoe is the best implement to use. It is also effective for weeding.

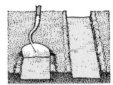

Making a flat bottomed drill

◄ **The Dutch Hoe**
The primary use of the Dutch hoe is in weeding, especially between rows of plants. It is used with a pushing motion to cut off weeds just below soil level.

Raking

As a tool for gathering up rubbish, a rake is one of the best. On the standard rake, the metal head is about 25–35cm(10–14in) wide with 4cm(1½in) long teeth; the Springbok has strong wire teeth about 30cm(1ft) long, spread out in a fan, with the end 4cm(1½in) bent over at right angles. There are also wooden rakes 90cm(3ft) wide, with wooden teeth 5cm(2in) long, and rubber-tined rakes.

The standard rake is also used for breaking up the surface soil of seedbeds into a fine crumb-like state, for levelling gravel paths, and covering seeds. The Springbok is used to clear lawns of refuse and dead moss; the wooden rake – a hay-rake – for collecting leaves and initial surface-soil levelling. Rubber-tined rakes are useful for leaf collection from lawns.

As well as the Springbok, there is now a wheeled rake for use on lawns, mainly to clear grass cuttings and fallen leaves, but it can also be used for removing dead grass. The advantage of this rake is that it can be drawn smoothly across a grass surface without pulling and tearing at the turf. It is, however, limited to use on grass.

USING RAKES

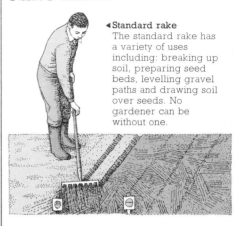

◀ **Standard rake**
The standard rake has a variety of uses including: breaking up soil, preparing seed beds, levelling gravel paths and drawing soil over seeds. No gardener can be without one.

◀ **Springbok rake**
Sometimes called the lawn rake because of its usual function of clearing leaves from lawns, the Springbok is valuable for clearing rubbish from all parts of the garden.

Ridging

This is a form of cultivation, done in the autumn, which exposes a greater area of soil to the weathering effects of rain, snow, frost and wind. It is especially good for heavy clay soils.

The site is divided into strips, about 60cm(2ft) wide, and a trench 1 spit deep and about 30cm(1ft) wide dug across the first strip, the soil being removed to the far end. Then the soil from the centre of a second trench is thrown forward into the centre of the first trench, but that from each side is thrown on top of it to form a ridge. The site will eventually consist of a succession of ridges. There are various other ways of forming ridges, but the one illustrated is easy to follow and not too messy in its operation. The resulting neatly ridged plot should present a rather pleasing appearance. Because ridging is of most benefit to heavy or clay soils, it tends to be very heavy work. It is good practice, therefore, to do the work when conditions are fine and dry and when the soil is at its most workable. This will mean ridging before the worst of the winter conditions, thus giving the additional benefit of exposing the soil to the maximum period of weathering.

HOW TO MAKE RIDGES

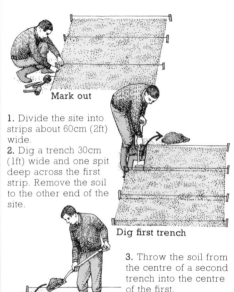

Mark out

1. Divide the site into strips about 60cm (2ft) wide.
2. Dig a trench 30cm (1ft) wide and one spit deep across the first strip. Remove the soil to the other end of the site.

Dig first trench

3. Throw the soil from the centre of a second trench into the centre of the first.
4. Throw the soil from each side of the second trench onto the soil already moved into the first.

Dig second trench

5. Continue up and down the strips until the plot is covered with ridges.

Continue across plot

45

Fertilizers

Fertilizers are substances containing concentrated plant foods. Plants use as food minerals such as iron, sulphur, phosphorus and many others, which they absorb in solution through their roots. These nutrients are present in the soil, but often there are not enough of them for the concentrated plant cover which is found in cultivation.

Also, many garden soils have been worked for many years, and so are short of nutrients, particularly the sandy or shingly soils, because rain washes the plant foods through the soil before the roots can absorb them.

Fertilizers may be the 'straights' which supply mainly one nutrient, such as sulphate of ammonia, which contains nitrogen, or compounds, which consist of the 'big three': nitrogen, phosphorus and potassium. These are the most important nutrients to a plant. Some are quick-acting, the inorganic kinds, which are absorbed in a few weeks. Others are slow-acting, such as hoof and horn meal – the organic derivatives, which release nutrient for several months.

The containers will give the rates of application and percentage of each nutrient present.

FERTILIZER CONSTITUENTS

The three main plant foods, nitrogen phosphorous and potassium, appear in a variety of forms. Those described here are the ones commonly used in gardens.

NITROGEN ●

The most rapidly effective of nitrogen containing fertilizers are sulphate of ammonia and nitrate of soda. Both should be effective within a matter of days. Sulphate of ammonia should not be used on acid soils and nitrate of soda will tend to increase the water holding capacity of the soil – particularly clay soils.

PHOSPHOROUS ●

Can be applied as calcium phosphate (bonemeal), but only on acid soils. Superphosphate is a commercial form which is suitable to all soils.

POTASSIUM ●

Commonly known as 'potash', this can be applied very simply in the form of wood ash from bonfires. More concentrated forms are: sulphate of potash (soluble in water), nitrate of potash (saltpetre) and kainit – a natural deposit quarried in Europe.

Manures

Manures consist mainly of the rotted remains of organic matter, animal or vegetable. Cow, pig and horse manure are very good; suitable alternatives are garden compost, seaweed, treated sewage sludge, spent mushroom compost and leafmould. All these supply some plant food.

However, the main purpose of manures is to keep the structure of the soil, i.e. the way in which the soil particles hold together, in a state which produces the optimum conditions of drainage and aeration for plant roots and so for plant health and growth. Without manure, the soil gradually becomes unsuitable for growth.

Peat is a good supplier of organic material, but contains no plant food beyond a little nitrogen. Other useful materials are sawdust, wood-shavings, shoddy, feathers, (these all take a year or two to rot down) and poultry deep litter. None of these is as good as the manures or composts mentioned earlier.

Rates of application for the conventional manures are 2½–8½kg per sq.m (5–18lb per sq.yd), using the lighter application on the clay-based soils, and the heavier on sandy or gravelly ones

Time to apply is autumn–winter, or early spring as a dug-in dressing; late spring or early autumn, as a top-dressing or mulch 2·5–7·5cm(1–3in) thick, round young or established plants.

ANIMAL MANURES

Horse
Contains small amounts of the vital plant foods. Should be applied liberally.

Cow
Seldom used where horse manure is available – being less easy to handle.

Pig
Wetter and denser than others, so do not apply to heavy soils. Nutritionally similar to horse manure.

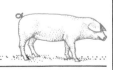

Poultry
Deep litter is richer in nitrogen and phosphorous than other animal manures.

Composts

Plants grown in containers do not have the space in which to develop their roots, as plants in the open ground do. Furthermore, there are great changes in the drainage and aeration of the soil in a container. The soil therefore has to be carefully blended from ingredients which ensure that roots can grow well, in spite of the limitation of space.

The soil-containing composts consist of good soil or loam, granulated peat and coarse sand, together with a compound fertilizer and chalk. The modern soilless composts contain peat and sand, and sometimes plant food and chalk. Some are especially for seeds, others for pot plants in general, and some are intended for cuttings. Composts can be bought ready mixed, or can be made up at home. Loam should be sterilised before mixing, and the mixture put through a sieve for the smaller plants.

Garden compost

As farm manures became very difficult to obtain, alternatives were sought, and it was found that garden compost was an excellent substitute. This is easily made, and also serves the purpose of getting rid of a good deal of unwanted

MAKING GARDEN COMPOST

1. Mark out the area and start the heap with waste vegetable matter.

2. Add a layer of manure or sulphate of ammonia.

3. Sprinkle with water.

4. Add a layer of soil about 2.5cm (1in deep).

5. Add another layer of vegetable matter.

6. Apply ground chalk or limestone, water, and add another layer of soil.

7. Continue building, adding manure or sulphate of ammonia to alternate layers, until the heap is about 1.3m (4ft) high.

8. Turn the heap over after 4–6 weeks, cover with a layer of soil and leave it until required.

Starting a compost heap Begin with waste vegetable matter from the kitchen and garden.

Continue building, adding manure to alternate layers

Soil
chalk/limestone

Waste vegetable matter

Soil

Manure

Waste vegetable matter

vegetation, which would otherwise have to be burnt.

Garden composts can be made from soft vegetative materials, such as leaves, grass clippings, weeds, young stems, flowers and so on. It should not contain woody stems, roots and tough vegetables stems (such as cabbage) unless crushed. Badly diseased or insect-ridden material should not be included, neither should particularly persistent weeds.

These materials are piled in a heap about 120cm(4ft) wide, 150cm(5ft) high and any convenient length. They should be added in layers about 15cm(6in) thick with alternating thin layers of animal manure or soil, or chalk, though the latter is not essential.

The base of the heap should consist of brushwood, so that air can go up through it. There should be moisture in it, and it should be enclosed with wooden walls, rigid plastic, black polythene sheet, or straw bales. Once finished, a covering should be put a few cm(inches) above it. A heap started in spring should be ready about 3 months later.

CONTAINING COMPOST

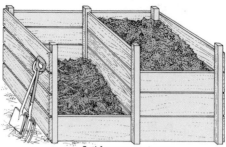

Notched post

A tidy compost area
Boards or planks slotted into notched posts make an ideal compost container. The compost benefits from air circulating through the spaces between the boards and the whole area is neatly enclosed and easy to manage.

Wire cage for grass cuttings
Grass cuttings and leaves are best kept in a wire cage which allows plenty of air to circulate.

Drainage

Drainage of the surplus moisture in the soil is extremely important. Not only is there no air, and therefore no oxygen in waterlogged soil, but the moisture gradually becomes more and more poisonous to plant roots. This is because the roots themselves give off waste products from the plant's metabolism-and because waste products and the decay of various soil organisms – bacterial, worms, fungi, etc. – also accumulate and become chemically dangerous.

Your soil will want draining if there is still water at the bottom of a hole 60cm(2ft) deep and square a week after prolonged rain. If there is a good deal of water, a soakaway, stone trenches or tile drains are needed.

The simplest method of improving soil drainage is to dig in grit, clinker, or strawy farm manure, and to use lime or gypsum.

When double digging, the bottom of the trench can have a layer of brushwood up to 30cm(1ft) deep put in it. Alternatively, trenches can be specially dug with a fall of 30cm(1ft) or more in 6m(20ft), and the lowest 25cm(10in) filled with stones or clinker, on which is placed 2cm(1in) or so of

TRENCHES/SOAKAWAYS

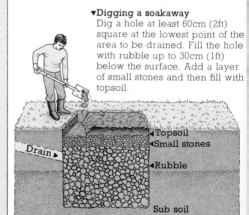

▼**Making a drainage trench**
The simplest method of making a trench specifically for drainage is to dig one with a fall of 30cm (1ft) in 6m (20ft). Fill the lowest 25cm (10in) with stones or clinker and cover with a 2.5cm (1in) layer of gravel. Then fill the trench with soil.

Topsoil
Gravel
Clinker
◄ Trench fall: 30cm (1ft) in 6m (20ft) ►

▼**Digging a soakaway**
Dig a hole at least 60cm (2ft) square at the lowest point of the area to be drained. Fill the hole with rubble up to 30cm (1ft) below the surface. Add a layer of small stones and then fill with topsoil.

Drain ►

◄ Topsoil
◄ Small stones

◄ Rubble

Sub soil

gravel or similar material, and the trench then filled in with soil.

Soakaways dug at the lowest point are also good: a hole is dug at least 60 × 60cm(2 × 2ft), deep enough to penetrate below the clay subsoil to more open soil below. Alternatively, it can have an outlet to a ditch or stream, via a tile-drain. The hole is filled with rubble, broken brick, stones, etc., to about 30cm(1ft) below the surface, and then filled in with smaller stones and topsoil.

The most thorough method of all for really badly drained soil, often used for lawns, is tile drainage. Sections of clay pipe about 30cm(1ft) long, are laid in line, but not quite touching, at the bottom of trenches 45–90cm(1½–3ft) deep, on a thin layer of small rubble, and just covered with similar material. Turves or brushwood are laid on top and topsoil used to fill in.

The trenches are dug in herringbone formation, with the tiles for the side drains 7·5cm(3in) in diameter and for the main drain 10cm(4in), which should lead to a ditch, etc. The fall should be 30cm in 27m (1ft in 90ft), with 3–9m(10–30ft) between branch drains. Use a spirit level to check that the rate of fall is consistent.

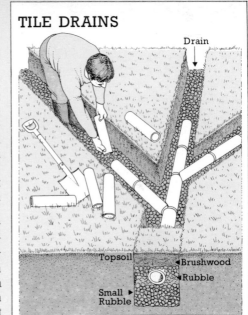

TILE DRAINS

Drain

Topsoil ◄ Brushwood
◄ Rubble
Small ► Rubble

Building the drain
Tile drainage is the best method for badly drained soils. Lay the main pipe of 10cm (4in) with branch pipes of 7.5cm (3in) diameter running into it at an angle of about 60°. The branch pipes should form a herringbone pattern and have a fall of 1 in 100. The pipes must be close but not touching. Cover with layers of rubble and brushwood and fill with topsoil.

■ Especially good for lawns

Soil analysis

The cultivation of strong healthy plants is largely dependent on a good soil structure. The ideal loam is rare, and most soils have a bias in one direction or another. Clues as to the type can be obtained from the feel and colour of it; the speed with which rain drains through it is another, and also the growth of plants. Use the table to help establish the type of soil you have in your garden.

Besides deciding on the structure of your soil, you will need to know its reaction, i.e. whether it has an acid or alkaline reaction. This is called the pH of the soil, and its value is determined by a scale which runs from 0–14. The centre of it, 7·0, is the neutral point; lower values are acid, higher, alkaline. Most plants grow best at a slightly acid pH, 6·5, and many garden soils are within the range 6·0–7·5.

Kits to test for these values can be obtained from garden shops and centres; they consist of an indicator solution which changes colour when mixed with the soil. The colours are then compared to a chart supplied with the kit, each shade or change in which corresponds to a particular pH value.

The kit will then advise how much lime to add, according to the reaction and the use for which the soil is required.

Chalk (calcium carbonate) or ground limestone are commonly used, the latter is slower-acting; both are put on in winter. Hydrated lime (calcium hydroxide) is quicker acting and can be used round plants. Gypsum (calcium oxide) does the same work in breaking the soil down as chalk, but it is neutral.

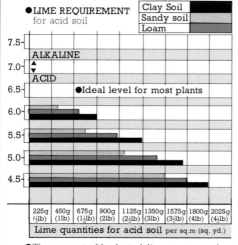

● LIME REQUIREMENT for acid soil

Clay Soil
Sandy soil
Loam

ALKALINE
ACID

●Ideal level for most plants

7.5 — 7.0 — 6.5 — 6.0 — 5.5 — 5.0 — 4.5 —

| 225g (½lb) | 450g (1lb) | 675g (1½lb) | 900g (2lb) | 1125g (2½lb) | 1350g (3lb) | 1575g (3½lb) | 1800g (4lb) | 2025g (4½lb) |

Lime quantities for acid soil per sq.m (sq. yd.)

●The amount of hydrated lime, or ground limestone, needed to raise pH to approximately 6.5

SOIL TYPE	DESCRIPTION	TREATMENT
HEAVY CLAY●	Feels sticky when wet; cracks badly when dry; grey or grey-brown; contains few stones but large flints may be present; puddles remain for many hours after rain	Add manure or garden compost; coarse sand at $3\frac{1}{2}$kg per sq.m. (7lb per sq. yd.); add lime if it is acid
SANDY●	Gritty when wet or dry; brown to light brown in colour; contains small stones; dries quickly and is easy to fork even after rain; plant growth pale and short	Add rotted organic matter in late winter
CHALKY●	Smooth but not sticky when wet; white to light brown; may contain large flints; subsoil white; topsoil shallow; drains well; plants may have yellowing leaves	Add rotted organic matter; do not dig too deeply
PEATY●	Springy and spongy; especially when wet; dark brown to black; virtually no stones; always moist, though surface will be dry in hot weather; much moss present	Spread lime to adjust natural acidity; drainage trenches may be necessary
LOAMY●	Neither gritty nor sticky, but open and workable; some stones; topsoil up to 60cm (2ft) deep; plant growth good and well-coloured; drains quite quickly	Correction of acidity or alkalinity may be all that is necessary
STONY●	May feel gritty and will contain many small and large stones; light in colour; shallow, with rock, chalk or clay subsoil; dries very quickly; plant growth sparse and pale	Add rotted organic matter in late winter; remove larger stones

Seed beds

The production of a fine soil surface which is suitable for sowing seeds is essential if seed germination is to be successful. The surface soil should resemble bread crumbs in its structure; it should be level, without bumps or hollows, and it should be evenly firm. There should not be any lumps of soil, stones, weeds or rubbish present.

Once the basic digging has been done, the soil is further broken up with a fork, and levelled as far as possible; at the same time all rubbish is cleared off.

Hoeing to break up remaining clods of soil is the next step, followed by firming – treading regularly and evenly when the surface soil is beginning to dry.

Finally the site is raked with a backwards and forwards motion, trying to avoid raking the larger crumbs to the edges, but either breaking them up or distributing evenly over the whole area.

At this stage, fertilizer can be sprinkled on by hand, and a second and final raking done crossways to the first.

Preparing the seed bed is best done when conditions are fairly settled and the soil is beginning to warm up. Prolonged heavy rain will ruin a good bed.

PREPARING A SEED BED

◄**Breaking-up**
Break-up the soil with a fork and level the bed as much as possible. Use the full depth of the fork on heavy soils.

Clear as you go►
Remove the larger stones, old roots and other rubbish as you progress with breaking-up the soil.

◄**Finishing off**
Hoe to break-up remaining lumps, tread the surface to make it even then rake.

Drills

A drill is a shallow furrow made in the soil in a straight line, in which seeds are sown. String is stretched the length of the row required, attached to a peg at each end of the row, and just above the soil. Using the string as a guide, the corner of the draw hoe is run along the soil, making the drill 6–19mm($\frac{1}{4}$–$\frac{3}{4}$in) deep.

Seeds are sown thinly in a line along the drill; this is 'continuous' sowing. 'Station' sowing consists of sowing 2 or 3 seeds at regular intervals, usually 5–7cm(2–3in).

For special seeds such as peas or broad beans, a very wide drill, or shallow trench is made, with a spade, to remove soil 5 or 7cm (2 or 3in) deep.

Another method of sowing is broadcast, a method in which the seed is scattered evenly by hand over the area to be covered.

After sowing, the soil is raked gently back over the seed, and firmed.

A lining of moist granulated peat or seed compost in the drills, and covering with cloches before and after sowing, will help to overcome weather problems.

PLANTING IN DRILLS

◀**Marking out**
Mark straight lines with the garden line and pins and make your drills with the corner of a draw hoe. This gives the usual v-shaped drill.

Sowing▲
Using either station sowing or continuous sowing, according to the variety, place the seeds into the drill.

◀**Finishing**
Rake the soil gently over the seeds and firm down with the back of the rake or with your feet.

Thinning

Seeds can be sown very thinly, but even so the resultant seedlings will need more space in which to grow. They are therefore removed, i.e. thinned or 'singled' in two stages. The first is as soon as they are large enough to handle, when 2 seed leaves and 1 true leaf are present. The number of seedlings left should be twice as many as will finally be required. The second is done some weeks later, when the leaves of the young plants are touching, to the final spacing.

Care should be taken to see that the roots of the retained seedlings are disturbed as little as possible and the soil should be firmed afterwards. If thinning in dry soil, watering in afterwards is advisable.

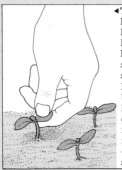

◀Thinning – first stage
Begin when 2 seed leaves and one true leaf are present. Before lifting, hold the seedling gently by a seed leaf.
Lifting▶
Using a plastic plant label or forked stick, gently prize up the roots. An unbroken root has a rounded tip – a broken one is square.

Pricking out

Seeds sown in containers also need more space than is available in the seed-tray. At the same stage of growth as that for first thinning, they are lifted and removed to a second seed-tray, in which they are planted $5 \times 5cm(2 \times 2in)$ apart.

They should be lifted with the roots intact as far as possible, using a label, metal widger or forked stick. It is particularly important that the tip of the main root is not broken; an unbroken tip is rounded, a broken one square.

When replanted, the stem should be buried up to the seed leaves. Pricked out plants should be watered with a rosed can, and put in a shady place for a day or two while they re-establish.

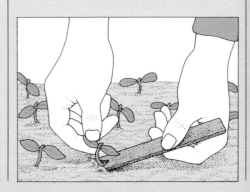

Transplanting

Transplanting refers to plants grown outdoors in the open ground; they may be young plants grown from seed, which need more space, or mature plants growing in an unsuitable site or soil. As with pricking out, transplanting has to be done with as little injury to the roots as possible.

Plants from seed are transplanted, when large enough to be handled without difficulty, from a seed-bed to their permanent position, e.g. brassicas; or to a nursery bed, e.g. biennials, Brompton stocks, polyanthus, pansies. They should be planted so that the lowest leaves are just above the soil surface.

Watering the plants the night before transplanting, removing to moist soil and planting in the evening, followed by watering in, will ensure the least check to the plants. It is almost impossible to transplant without some effect, however, on the development of the plant. Obviously, this can be a more detrimental effect with vegetables than most other plants. The best insurance is to give the plants plenty of water – it is very easy to underestimate the amount that young vegetable plants need.

TRANSPLANTING METHODS

Lift and separate the plants carefully, making sure that the root ball is intact. Use your fingers for separating plants.

Make holes with a dibber and place a seedling into each hole. Be very careful not to break or crush the root ball.

Fill the hole and firm gently around the plant with your fingers. Make sure that the soil around the stem is level.

57

Weeding

Control of weeds is important because they absorb plant food and water, and use space and light. However, a low weed cover is useful because the soil remains moister beneath it. Even so, they should be destroyed before they flower, either with weedkiller, by digging in or removing completely.

They can be hand-weeded or hoed out, preferably when seedlings, and seeds can be prevented from germinating by mulches of organic matter, black plastic sheet or stones.

Chemical weedkillers are effective. Paraquat and diquat combined will destroy seedlings and annual weeds if sprayed on to leaves and stems. There is no effect on the roots, because these chemicals do not act below soil level.

Glyphosate is also sprayed on to the top growth, and will destroy also perennial and deep-rooting weeds.

Both these chemicals can be used round cultivated plants provided the solution does not contact their leaves or stems; there are special sprinkler bar attachments for watering cans which make this easier. Attacking the weeds, either with chemicals or by hand, when they are just beginning to make new growth gives them the greatest check

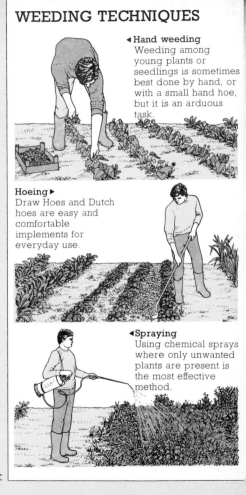

WEEDING TECHNIQUES

◄ **Hand weeding**
Weeding among young plants or seedlings is sometimes best done by hand, or with a small hand hoe, but it is an arduous task.

Hoeing ►
Draw Hoes and Dutch hoes are easy and comfortable implements for everyday use.

◄ **Spraying**
Using chemical sprays where only unwanted plants are present is the most effective method.

Mulching

Mulches, or top dressings, consist of layers of material on the soil surface around plants. Those which consist of rotted organic matter, such as manure or garden compost, or straw, lawn mowings, leaves, sawdust and so on, can be anything from 2·5–12cm (1–5in) thick depending on their purpose and the type of soil. They may also be of stones, sand or plastic sheeting – which may even be perforated.

Mulching has a variety of important uses: it may be to keep moisture in the soil, to stop the germination and growth of weeds, to improve the soil structure, to supply nutrient, to retain soil warmth, or protect plants.

Applications should be in late spring or early summer; on to moist, clean, weed free soil – or early to late autumn. At the latter time, organic matter is best, because it supplies food and humus.

Protective mulches are used through the cold months on tender plants which die down in winter, and whose crowns and roots are vulnerable to frost. Dried bracken, straw, peat or leaves may all be used, piled at least 15cm(6in) thick over and around the crowns of the plants. When using plastic sheeting remember to peg it or weight it down.

MULCHING TECHNIQUES

The type of mulch you use in your garden depends to some extent upon the type of plant, and partly upon the time of year. Spring mulches, which are used chiefly to preserve moisture, check weed growth and provide some plant food, would normally consist of compost or rotted organic matter. The mulch should be spread evenly over the entire root area of the plant and vary from a thickness of 5cm (2in) for some shrubs and perennials, to 7.5cm (3in) for roses and 10cm (4in) for young trees. Where shrubs or perennials are grouped together, it is worthwhile to cover the entire bed with the mulch. The plastic sheeting mulch is most often used for young vegetables, where conservation of warmth is most vital.

Feeding

A plant can obtain some of its 'food' from the atmosphere – oxygen and water – which can be combined inside it during daylight so as to produce other substances of use to its metabolism.

It also obtains nutrient from the soil in the form of mineral particles of such elements as iron, sulphur, potassium, etc. These are usually present as compounds – salts combined with other minerals, and the plant roots can take them in, provided they are in solution.

Liquid fertilizers, containing these mineral foods in varying proportions, act very quickly but temporarily. They must be applied frequently, at 3–14 day intervals, during the season of growth, i.e. not in winter. They are generally watered on to the soil.

Foliar feeds can also be used. These are sprayed on to the leaves, through which they are absorbed, and they are even quicker acting, and less long lasting.

Powder fertilizers are put on dry, by hand or with a fertilizer distributor, and raked or forked in to the top few centimetres (inches). If the soil is dry at the time of application they should be watered in. Remember that excessive applications are not beneficial.

FEEDING METHODS

◄ **Liquid fertilizers**
Although liquid plant foods are quickly effective they have only a short term benefit and must be applied frequently. Pour on to the base of the plant avoiding contact with the leaves.

Foliar feeds ►
These are even more immediate in effect and shorter lasting than liquid fertilizers. They can be sprayed on to the foliage or applied with a watering can.

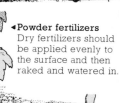

◄ **Powder fertilizers**
Dry fertilizers should be applied evenly to the surface and then raked and watered in.

Watering

Most plants consist very largely of water. Those which live in almost permanently dry conditions have adapted so that they can store water for months if necessary.

If plants lack moisture, they also lack nutrient, which can only be absorbed in solution. Lack of water therefore means a starved plant as well as a wilting one.

Plants that endure a period of drought, followed by heavy rain or watering, make a great amount of new growth very quickly. Vegetables and fruit do so more quickly than the root, tuber or fruit can accommodate. Hence skins split, roots and tubers crack and secondary growth occurs, causing malformation.

Outdoor watering should start after only a few days of hot dry weather, unless the soil was very wet initially. It should be continued regularly until the drought breaks, applying the water as a gentle spray through rosed watering cans, sprinklers or spray attachments to hoses. Each application should continue for about 2 hours, evening or early morning, and be repeated about 4–7 days later depending on temperature.

WATERING TECHNIQUES

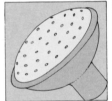

◄ Using cans
The galvanised metal can with a copper rose is still the best device for watering in after sowing, planting or transplanting. They usually hold about 1 ll (2½ gal.) of water.

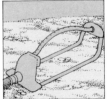

◄ Sprinklers
Using a sprinkler is the only way to simulate the effect of rainfall. Sprinklers provide a gentle, consistent spray and can be used for up to 2 hours in the same place.

Frost protection

Plants, even hardy ones, can be killed by frost, so it is advisable to have some form of frost protection easily to hand. Mid and late spring frosts, and early autumn ones, often do the most damage, because they are unexpected. Night is the time when the temperature drops most, so a useful form of indirect protection is a maximum and minimum thermometer. The night readings will put you on the alert in good time.

Protection from varying degrees of frost can consist of: 15cm(6in) deep mulches over the crowns of plants, held down with bent bamboo canes or wires; cloches, polythene tunnels or frames; sacking or newspaper on top of frames; fibre-glass, straw, or sacking lagging round the outside of containers; polythene sheet lining to greenhouses; artifical heating for frames and greenhouses; straw, paper or sacking over plants or bushes.

It is wise, when planning your garden, to take careful not of the parts of the site which are most and least affected by frost – and plant accordingly. Never place susceptible plants at the lowest part of the garden; cold air is heavier than warm and will collect at the bottom of slopes.

FROST PROTECTION

Newspaper
The lights of cold frames can be covered with newspaper or sacking, but remember to remove the lagging during daylight.

Plastic
Sheets or sacks of plastic can be drawn around posts to protect taller plants.

Mulches
Mulching with straw or peat can help to prevent frost attacking at soil level.

Wind protection

Newly planted shrubs and trees, especially conifers, are particularly vulnerable to wind, but even established ones, and of course the slightly tender kinds, will all appreciate something between them and a north-east draught.

Permanent wind protection can be provided by hedges or screens of deciduous and evergreen trees or shrubs – holly, yew, beech, thorn, cypresses and privet are all good. If they cannot be provided all round a site, they should protect it at least from the north and east.

Temporary forms of protection can consist of: sheets of plastic, sacking or 1·2cm(½in) mesh windbreak netting attached to poles placed round plants, wire netting folded double with bracken or straw between the sheets, or 6mm(¼in) Rokolene plastic windbreak netting used as a tent or blanket.

On open, windy sites, many plants which do not normally require support may need staking. This applies particularly to the taller growing vegetables and border plants – anything, in fact, which grows to 60cm (2ft) or more. Bamboo canes, or posts and wires, will suffice for most plants.

WIND PROTECTION

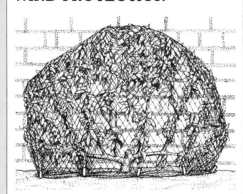

Netting
Fine mesh netting will give considerable protection to fruit trees in quite severe conditions.

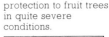

Bracken tent
A conical structure of wire and cane stuffed with bracken gives both wind and frost protection.

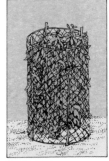

Wire cage
If the mesh is fairly fine, a wire cage is good protection for tall plants and saplings.

Seeds and germination

If seeds are to germinate at all they must have moisture, oxygen and a suitable temperature, which is usually 16°C (60°F) or above. Many will not germinate unless in the dark, but there are some that require light. Once germinated, the seedling roots need nutrient, especially phosphorus. The presence or absence of this mineral can make or break the life and health of the mature plant.

Many seeds will germinate in lower temperatures than the optimum but do so increasingly slowly, according to the decrease in the temperature, until it becomes so low that they remain dormant.

For good seed germination, supply the requirements stated; if they are sown in containers use sterilized loam in a soil-containing compost. Sow sparsely and evenly, using the finger and thumb of one hand to take seed from the palm of the other hand.

Cover them with their own depth of finely sifted moist soil or compost, and firm down. Very fine seed can be bulked with coarse sand to make sowing easier. Water containers from the base and, in general, cover with black polythene sheet or glass and brown paper, though opaque plastic sheet is said to give as good, and sometimes better, results.

Outdoors, the seeds must have a moist, warm soil with a fine tilth. Dry soil, cold soil, very wet soil, an uneven and lumpy seed-bed, and too deep or too shallow sowing will result in no, or

Collecting seeds
When harvesting vegetables allow some plants to run to flower and collect the seeds for next season's sowing.

lings.

Seeds should be ripe when sown:
generally this means that the best time
to sow is soon after they would naturally
be released by the parent plant.
However, some need a period of cold
after ripening – mainly the shrubs,
trees and alpine plants. These can be
stratified in winter, i.e. placed in layers
in moist peat or sand in a container such
as a pan, and left outdoors all winter,
protected from marauding mice by
wire netting.

Seeds which are difficult to germinate can often be encouraged by
chipping, e.g. sweetpeas. Nicking their
hard outer covering with a sharp knife
will ensure germination. Others can be
soaked for 6–24 hours in warm water
before sowing.

Annuals, biennials, half-hardy annuals and vegetables are the plants
usually grown from seed. Herbaceous
perennials, rock plants, bulbs, shrubs
and trees can all be grown from seed as
well; the bulbs can take 3–6 years to
flower, shrubs and trees even longer,
and of course there is no guarantee that
plants grown from home-saved seed
will be exactly like their parent.

SOWING IN CONTAINERS

1. Sow seeds evenly and sparingly, using finger
and thumb.
2. Cover them with their own depth of sifted
moist soil.
3. Cover with black polythene sheet.

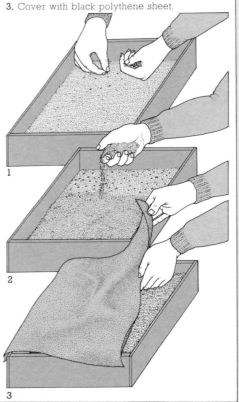

Cuttings

This is a very common method of vegetative propagation, which can be used for the great majority of plants. It makes use of the fact that the response of stem tissue to injury is to produce roots, especially at certain points on the stem.

Cuttings usually consist of short lengths of stem from young shoots produced in the current growing season. They can be 5–38cm(2–15in) long, and consist of the end of the shoot, rather than the base; they should not have flowered or have flower buds on them.

Tip or soft cuttings are short, 7–10cm(3–4in) long. They are taken before the stem has had time to ripen and harden. The cut is made cleanly just below a leaf-joint, and the bottom leaf or pair of leaves cut off close to the stem.

The cutting is then put into a hole in the compost at the side of a pot, to about half its length, making sure that the base rests on the compost. It is firmed in sufficiently well to ensure that a gentle tug to one of the leaves does not shift it, and then watered.

A 9cm(3½in) pot will take 3–5 cuttings, which are then covered with an inflated transparent polythene bag, and put in a warm shady place. When a cutting

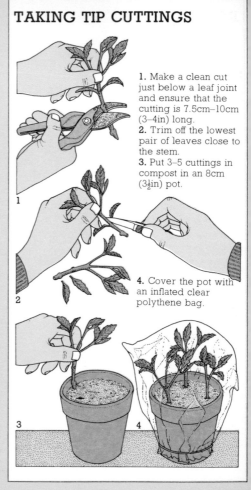

TAKING TIP CUTTINGS

1. Make a clean cut just below a leaf joint and ensure that the cutting is 7.5cm–10cm (3–4in) long.
2. Trim off the lowest pair of leaves close to the stem.
3. Put 3–5 cuttings in compost in an 8cm (3½in) pot.

4. Cover the pot with an inflated clear polythene bag.

ROOT AND LEAF CUTTINGS

Cutting roots

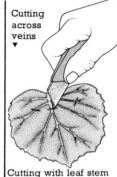

Cutting across veins ▼

Cutting with leaf stem ▼

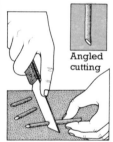

Angled cutting

Root cuttings
Cuttings can be taken from plants with fleshy roots. Cut the roots into pieces 2.5–7cm (1–3in) long making a slanting cut to indicate the bottom. Plant with the slanting cut downwards.

Leaf cuttings
Propagation from leaf cuttings is possible with very many plants. Some, such as *begonias*, are laid on potting compost after cutting across the main veins. Others, like *African violets*, are planted with the leaf stem.

begins to lengthen, it will have rooted, and can be potted separately as soon as root tips appear through drainage holes.

Time taken to root can be a few days or a few weeks. Soft cuttings generally root best in spring or early summer; they need warmth to encourage rooting. Hormone rooting compounds may also help. Herbaceous plants including dahlias, chrysanthemums, lupins, pelargoniums, delphiniums, pot and house plants, and some shrubs, will root from tip cuttings.

Semi-hardwood or half-ripe cuttings are taken in early–late summer. The stems by then have begun to harden and become pale brown from the base though still green and soft for about half their length. They are about 5–15cm(2–6in) long, and are treated in the same way as tip cuttings. Shrubs, including heathers, conifers, pelargoniums and other bedding plants can be grown from half-ripe cuttings.

Ripe or hardwood cuttings are taken in mid autumn, give or take 2 to 3 weeks, using shoots 23–38cm(9–15in) long. They can be rooted outdoors, in a sheltered place, or in a cold frame.

A narrow V-shaped trench is made,

its depth being equal to about half the length of the cutting. A shallow layer of coarse sand is put in the bottom, and the cuttings put on to it, spaced 10cm(4in) or so apart, lying against the side. The trench is then filled in with good soil or compost.

Sometimes rooting occurs before winter, and the cuttings then become dormant until spring, or the base of the cutting callouses over until spring, and then produces roots. Rooted hardwood cuttings should not be transplanted until the autumn after they were taken.

Roses, shrubs, bush fruits and trees can be increased by hardwood cuttings.

Cuttings of leaves are sometimes used, mostly for tender plants, e.g. African violet, begonia, or sansevieria.

Begonia leaves are laid flat on the surface of a sandy compost. About six 1·2cm($\frac{1}{2}$in) long cuts are made across the main veins, and the leaf weighed down with small stones, or pinned down with wire hooks. The pan is put in a polythene bag, in a warm, shady place. Plantlets will grow from the cuts.

Sansevieria leaves are transversely cut into sections about 5cm(2in) long, and half buried upright in sandy com-post. Temperature needs to be about 24°C(75°F). Individual African violet leaves, with their stems attached, are put singly into soilless compost, to about half the length of the stem, co-vered with a polythene bag and put in a warm shady place. Tiny leaves will grow up through the compost from the base of the stem, and there may finally be several plantlets formed.

Root cuttings will also produce new plants. They are taken in winter, mostly from herbaceous perennials with fleshy roots, e.g. verbascum, hollyhock, phlox, romneya, oriental poppy, gail-lardia, anchusa, sea lavender and bouvardia.

The roots are cut into pieces 2·5–7·5cm(1–3in) long, and placed in pans of sandy compost, either flat on the surface, or buried upright, with the tops just below the surface, and then wa-tered. A slanting cut at the bottom end of the root will ensure that they go in the right way up.

After spending the winter in an un-heated greenhouse or cold frame, during which time they should be wa-tered moderately, they will have pro-duced substantial shoots and can be planted in the herbaceous border.

Division

Dividing plants is one of the simplest methods of vegetative propagation. The best times to do it are spring and autumn. Herbaceous perennials are often increased like this, either by cutting, splitting, or levering apart with two forks back to back in the centre of the crown.

Separating the new side bulbs, or offsets, from parent bulbs of daffodils, tulips, hyacinths, etc., is another form of division. These can be planted separately to flower two or more years later.

Plants with tuberous roots can also be divided, ensuring that each piece of plant has a tuber with 'eyes' or dormant buds on it, e.g. dahlias. Some tubers can be cut into pieces, e.g. begonia or cyclamen.

Dividing large plants
Lever apart tough root clumps with two forks placed back to back.

Runners

Runners are a method of vegetative propagation which the plant produces naturally without any help from man. Each runner consists of a length of stem from the plant's crown, at the end of which is a plantlet. This produces roots and a further length of stem with another plantlet at the end.

If the stem is pegged down to the soil close to the plantlet it will be encouraged to root and, when firmly established, the runner can be cut. The plantlet is then lifted some weeks later and planted in its permanent position.

Strawberries are easily increased like this; other examples are London Pride, creeping bugle, and chlorophytum (spider plant).

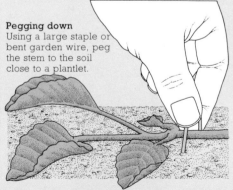

Pegging down
Using a large staple or bent garden wire, peg the stem to the soil close to a plantlet.

Layers

Plants which can be increased by layering tend to be those which produce stems close to soil level, or which can easily be pulled down to it. Some shrubs and roses, bush fruits and border carnations can all be propagated like this, at more or less any time between late spring and early autumn.

Clematis are an exception they are layered between mid autumn and early spring. Also, two-year-old shoots must be used for clematis, whereas one-year-old shoots are preferred for the woody plants. Carnation shoots need only be a few weeks old, and must be non-flowering.

Basically, layering consists of making a sloping cut upwards, partially through the underside of a stem, and pinning the stem down into the soil. The cut should be made on the underside of the branch or stem, the cut surface then pegged down into a sandy compost or good loam, and the end of the shoot supported vertically with a stake or cane. Roots will form from the cut and the plant can be detached in a few months, and planted 12–18 months after first layering. Layering is more effective than taking cuttings where the plant concerned has a woody stem.

LAYERING TECHNIQUE

A great many shrubs can be propagated by this method which is also suitable for soft fruits.

Make a sloping cut partly through the underside of a branch or stem and peg the cut surface into a sandy compost or a good loam.

Roots will be formed from the cut, but the process takes several months and it is not generally possible to transplant the new plant within a year.

Making cut

Peg down at cut

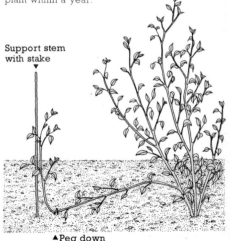
Support stem with stake

▲Peg down

Budding

Budding is a form of *grafting* mostly used for propagating roses. A bud from the plant to be increased, with a sliver of bark and tissue attached, is grafted on to the rootstock, close to soil level for bush roses, 120–150cm(4–5ft) for standards. Mid summer is the time to do it.

A T-shaped cut is made in the bark of the stock, the leg of the T being about 2cm($\frac{3}{4}$in) long. A bud from the middle of a shoot that has already flowered is then cut off, with a shield of bark and wood about 2·5cm(1in) long at the back of it. The sliver of wood is pulled off, leaving a small knob in the back of the bud; if this is pulled out too, the bud will not take.

The ends of the shield are trimmed, the leaf cut off so that a small piece of stem is left, and the bud inserted at the top of the T-cut by lifting up the bark with the flat end of the knife handle. It is pushed down as far as it will go, with the flaps of bark back in place, and the leaf stem protruding. It is then bound with raffia or plastic budding tape.

The following early spring, if the bud is showing signs of swelling or sprouting, the stock is cut back to about 2·5cm(1in) above the bud, and a cane supplied to support the budded shoot.

BUDDING TECHNIQUE

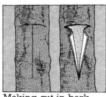

Making cut in bark

In budding roses, first make a T-shaped cut in the bark of the rootstock – close to soil level on bush roses, 120–150cm (4–5ft) above on standards.

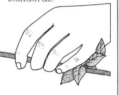

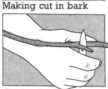

Cutting bud

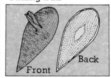

Front   Back

Cut a bud from a stem which has flowered, leaving a shield of bark and a small piece of wood behind the bud. Strip off the piece of wood, trim the bark, and cut off the leaf leaving a small piece of stem.

Inserting bud

Lifting the bark with the knife handle, insert the bud at the top of the T-cut and push it down as far as possible.

Binding up

Making sure that the piece of leaf stem is protruding, replace the flaps of bark and bind with raffia or plastic tape.

71

Pruning-basic principles

Pruning of woody plants is done to encourage the production of the new growth, flowers and fruits, and to remove dead or diseased shoots or branches. It also keeps the plant within the space available if it proves to be larger than was expected.

The growth pruned is nearly always the most recent, the one-year-old shoots. This has green bark in its first growing season, which gradually turns brown from the base until, by autumn, the tip is mature and brown also.

When pruning, remember that severe cutting back encourages growth in a healthy plant, little or light cutting produces the opposite result. Hard pruning means the cutting-off of most of the new growth to leave about $\frac{1}{4}\frac{1}{3}$ of it. Moderate cutting will leave about $\frac{1}{2}\frac{2}{3}$, light pruning will only remove the tip to about $\frac{1}{4}$ the length of the shoot.

But hard pruning can also mean cutting all the new growth by about half; moderate pruning can mean cutting half the total number of new shoots back hard, and light pruning can mean cutting some of the shoots by about half, or a few, back hard.

When starting to prune, take out first obviously dead shoots, those with disease, shoots markedly shorter and thinner than the rest, shoots which crowd or cross others, and shoots growing into the centre. This is standard pruning. Then deal with the remainder, trying to let light and air into the centre of the plant, and also keeping its natural shape as far as possible.

Make pruning cuts cleanly, and always use a razor-sharp knife or secateurs. Cut back to just above a bud pointing to the outside of the plant, not too close. However, do not leave an appreciable snag. Make sure the cut is sloping, away from the bud. Vegetative buds are long and pointed, flower and fruit buds are round and fat.

Pruning tools ▶
The most essential item in the pruning kit is a pair of pruning shears (secateurs). They vary in design to some extent but not in application. Make sure that you buy a strong and well-sprung type. Pruning knives are necessary for more delicate work and saws for tree pruning. A pen knife is a useful item to have in your pocket when doing any garden job. Flower shears will cut stems at the same time as retaining the severed part – so you cannot drop the flower.

■See also page 80–81

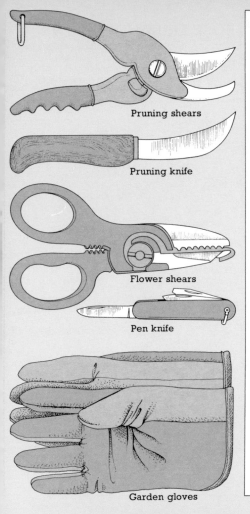

Pruning shears

Pruning knife

Flower shears

Pen knife

Garden gloves

GENERAL INFORMATION

Light prune

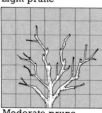

Moderate prune

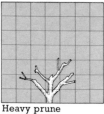

Heavy prune

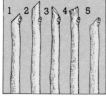

Degrees of pruning
Light pruning usually means removing the tip and, perhaps, as much as $\frac{1}{4}$ of the shoot. Moderate pruning will remove $\frac{1}{3}-\frac{1}{2}$ of the new growth and hard pruning will cut back $\frac{2}{3}-\frac{3}{4}$. There are other systems of pruning, in some the shoots are cut back to varying degrees, but almost all pruning is carried out on the most recent growth.

Correct pruning
Always use a very sharp knife and make smooth, clean cuts. Cut back to just above a bud, but not too close. Use the diagram, below left, as a guide.
1. Correct
2. Too far from bud
3. Wrong angle
4. Ragged cut
5. Too close
Remember that flower and fruit buds are long and pointed, vegetative buds are round and fat

73

Roses

Modern bush roses (hybrid teas) will give the best garden display if pruned moderately. Those of the floribunda type will do best with a mixture of pruning, tipping the youngest growth, pruning the new shoots of the middle aged growth moderately, and removing one or two of the oldest shoots at ground level, when about four or five years old. Treat standards as hybrid teas. Time to prune is about early spring, or just before growth starts.

At planting time, cut all the stems down hard, so that about 10–15cm (4–6in) of each is left.

Ramblers are pruned in early – mid autumn. Cut off completely at ground level the shoots which have flowered in the summer, and tie the new ones in their place. At planting time, cut the stems to 60–90cm(2–3ft), if not already done by the nursery.

Climbers are pruned in early spring. Cut dead tips and other dead growth off, cut off flowered shoots, and cut sideshoots which come off the main stem, to leave about 10cm(4in) of stem. At planting time, do not prune except to remove dead tips. Generally speaking, the severest pruning of roses is reserved for those grown for exhibition.

ROSE PRUNING TIPS

◀Bush/standard roses
In general, a moderate pruning is required but the youngest growth should just be tipped. Prune the middle growth moderately and cut back the old growth to ground level.

◀Ramblers
Prune in autumn and remove completely all shoots which have flowered in the summer. Tie new ones in their place.

◀Climbers
Prune in early spring cutting off all tips and dead growth and the flowered shoots. Cut sideshoots to about 10cm (4in) of the stem

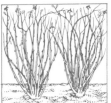

◀Shrub roses
Shrub roses need no regular pruning. Occasionally dead growth, crowded or crossing shoots can be removed, preferably in spring. Do not prune at planting time.

Shrubs

For pruning purposes, flowering shrubs fall into three sections. Those which flower in spring and up to the end of early summer are pruned as soon as flowering has finished. The flowered shoots are cut off, either completely or back to a strong new shoot. Pruning should be fairly moderate.

Those which flower from mid summer to mid autumn are pruned in spring, when growth is starting, and are pruned fairly hard, again cutting off flowered growth, any dead shoots.

Winter-flowering shrubs are pruned in spring, fairly lightly; little is needed, because these shrubs tend to grow rather slowly.

The remaining shrubs, mainly evergreens, need only have the standard pruning done occasionally or the removal of shoots which spoil their shape, generally in spring. If shrubs are grown for their berries, a balance between keeping berrying growth, and encouraging new, should be aimed at.

All shrubs are considerably improved by having the standard pruning done, even if no other cutting is done, otherwise they tend to get cluttered with unnecessary growth and flower less well.

WHEN TO PRUNE SHRUBS

FLOWERING SEASON	SHRUB	PRUNING SEASON
Spring to mid summer	Ceanothus Kerria Ribes Spiraea	After flowering has finished
Mid summer to autumn	Buddleia Caryopteris Clerodendrum Hydrangea	Spring
Winter to early spring	Chimonathus Cornus Forsythia Hamamelis	Spring, immediately after flowering

Climbers

Climbers follow the same principles, with the additional need to keep them within bounds. The large-flowered, mid to late summer-flowering clematis are pruned in late winter, very hard; they can in fact be sheared straight across at about 90cm(3ft) from the ground.

Early summer-flowering large-flowered hybrids can have the top 10 or 15cm(4 or 6in) removed at the same time of the year, cutting to just above a pair of dormant buds, or they can be left alone and cut hard back after flowering every few years.

Wisteria can also be left to its own devices, or pruned in late summer so as to cut the new shoots back to 5 leaves, and then in winter cut again so that one or two dormant buds remain on each new stem. As in all pruning, cuts should be made cleanly and close to a main branch, or just above a growing bud. Any resultant wounds should be treated with a wound dressing. Evergreen shrubs can be pruned hard in late spring but should never be cut back in winter. Trim them throughout the summer to maintain the required shape. Deciduous shrubs grown for foliage, should be pruned in winter.

PRUNING CLIMBERS

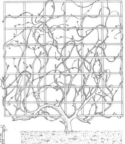

Clematis ▶
Prune the large flowered, mid-late summer flowering clematis very hard in late winter. Cut straight across 1m(3ft) from the ground.

◀Large flowered hybrids
These can be left alone for a few seasons and then cut back hard. Otherwise, just remove the tips each year.

Wisteria ▶
This shrub need not be pruned regularly, but if it is cut back the pruning should be in two stages: cut the new shoots back to 5 leaves in late summer, and cut again in winter leaving 2 dormant buds on each stem.

Ornamental trees

Ornamental trees do not need regular pruning, but they may need surgery, if a branch is damaged, broken off or diseased. In general, it is best to ask a professional tree surgeon to do the necessary cutting.

For small trees, branches can be removed by first making an under-cut partially through the branch about 60cm(2ft), or any convenient length from the trunk of the parent branch. A second cut is made partially through the upper side 2·5cm(1in) or so away from the first. This removes the branch, and then a third cut is made through the junction with the parent stem, and flush with it. This prevents the bark tearing on the parent stem. Early winter is the best time to do it, though work can be done in summer if it is unavoidable.

If trees are outgrowing their space, they can be pollarded. With this technique, the branches or shoots are cut back to the top of the trunk, every few years. A form of this is lopping, in which the shoots or boughs are cut back so as to leave stubs. Lime, plane, poplar, plane willow, elm and horse chestnut will survive this treatment well. Any wounds resulting from pruning should be treated with Stockholm tar.

REMOVING BRANCHES

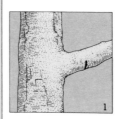
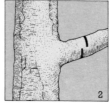
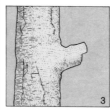
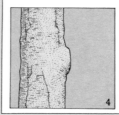

Early winter is the best time to do this job, though it may be necessary at other times of year if a branch has been damaged or become diseased. The technique described here is designed to remove the branch without any damage to the main stem or trunk.

1. Make a cut through the underside of the branch which is to be removed about 60cm (2ft) from the parent branch or trunk.
2. Make a second cut partially through the upper side of the branch about 2.5cm (1in) away from the first.
3. .As the cuts come close together, the branch will fall away but without stripping the bark from the trunk.
4. Make a third cut through the junction of the branch and the parent trunk and flush with it. Trim the cut and paint .it with Stockholm tar

Hedges

Formal deciduous hedges are clipped in mid-late summer; evergreens, including conifers, towards the end of late summer or in early autumn. If very quick growing, such as box, *Lonicera nitida*, etc., they will need clipping two or three times from late spring onwards.

Hedges which need rejuvenating can be cut down hard in spring, but conifers do not take kindly to this, and are better replanted. All quick-growing hedge plants are cut down hard to leave 10 or 12cm(4 or 5in) after planting, the remainder being tipped.

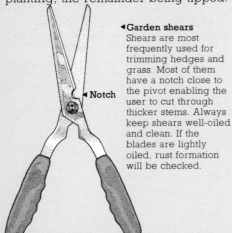

◄ **Garden shears**
Shears are most frequently used for trimming hedges and grass. Most of them have a notch close to the pivot enabling the user to cut through thicker stems. Always keep shears well-oiled and clean. If the blades are lightly oiled, rust formation will be checked.

◄ **Notch**

Fruit bushes and canes

Blackcurrants can be pruned in late summer or late autumn – early winter. They fruit on shoots produced in the previous growing season, so pruning aims at encouraging new growth.

Fruited shoots are cut hard, either at ground level, or low down, to just above the point at which a strong new shoot is growing. Remove all the weak sideshoots from the centre of the bush, and cut off completely the low-growing shoots, otherwise they get trodden on at picking time.

At planting time, cut down to leave 5 or 7·5cm(2 or 3in) of each stem.

Redcurrants and gooseberries fruit on two-year-old growth. Prune redcurrants late autumn – mid winter by cutting back the tips of the main shoots to remove a quarter of their length, and the side shoots hard to leave a short length of stem with one or two buds on it.

At planting time, cut back each shoot hard to leave three or four buds, the top one facing outwards. Repeat this in the second and third years.

Prune gooseberries at the same time of year by reducing the main shoots to about half their length, and the side-shoots to $\frac{1}{4}-\frac{1}{2}$, so that there is sufficient space to ensure that the picker's hands are not scratched. Always cut to an upper bud, and don't hesitate to cut crowded growth away altogether.

At planting time, prune as for red-currants and similarly in the second and third years.

Cane fruits are all pruned to remove the fruited growth completely. The old canes of raspberries are cut off at ground level after fruiting, and about five of the strongest new ones on each plant tied in. The rest are cut away.

Blackberries, loganberries, and hybrid berries are also pruned when they have fruited, and the new growth trained in separately in a fan shape. Three to four canes is sufficient for each plant.

At planting time, all the cane fruits are cut back to leave about 23–30cm (9–12in) of stem.

None of the bush or cane fruits should be allowed to fruit in the first summer planting. Cutting back severely at planting time, thus preventing the first year fruit from forming, concentrates the growth into the young shoots which will bear fruit in the second year. Subsequently the fruiting branches should be removed.

PRUNING BUSHES/CANES

Loganberries

Blackberries

Blackcurrants

Raspberries

Gooseberries

FRUIT	PRUNING SEASON	NOTES
Blackcurrants	Late summer or late autumn	Prune fruited shoots hard
Redcurrants	Late autumn to mid winter	Tips of main shoots; side shoots hard.
Gooseberries	Late summer to mid winter	Cut main and side shoots to about half
Loganberries Blackberries	After fruiting	Cut out fruited shoots
Raspberries	After fruiting	Cut out fruited shoots and the weakest new growth

Fruit trees

Apples and pears fruit naturally on shoots three years old, but restricted forms will fruit on younger growth. Bush forms are pruned in winter, while dormant. Moderate pruning is preferred, to leave about half the new shoots unpruned, and the remainder cut back by half, spreading this evenly over the tree. This will give the right balance between fruiting and vegetative growth.

However, it will need to be varied, according to the variety, the soil, the climate and the weather, and the feeding programme. The best results will come with experience of your own trees and garden. Some pear varieties have a markedly upright habit of growth which should be counteracted as far as possible, by cutting to side or under buds. Pears also have a greater tendency than other fruit trees to develop an excessive number of spurs. These have to be reduced in order to maintain the quality of the fruit. They can be kept under control by regular thinning and cutting back. On the whole, pears probably require more pruning than other fruit trees and are not so easy to look after as apples.

Cordons, espaliers and other restricted forms are partially pruned in mid–late summer by cutting sideshoots to five leaves, and sub-sideshoots to three leaves, not counting the basal cluster of leaves. In winter, these shoots are then cut to three and one bud respectively. The leading shoots are kept cut within the space available.

Bush plums, greengages and cherries are hardly pruned at all, except for the standard cutting, and some tipping of new growth. This is done after picking, from early to late summer.

No fruit trees are pruned after planting, but from the second to the fourth year after planting, pruning is aimed at producing and developing the framework of main branches on which the fruit will be carried.

There should be three or four good new shoots by the second winter, evenly spaced on the main stem. These are cut back hard, to outward pointing buds where possible, and weak shoots are cut right off. In the third and fourth winters this is repeated, removing completely shoots which are obviously going to be too close when mature branches. Remember that regular pruning is the key to good quality fruit.

EQUIPMENT

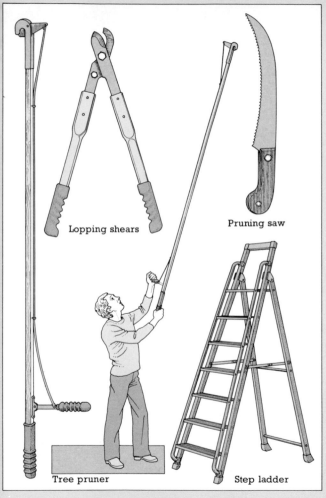

Lopping shears

Pruning saw

Tree pruner

Step ladder

Tree pruning equipment
The most important items in the tree pruning kit are the saw and a pair of step ladders. Pruning saws come in many shapes and sizes but the most common, and the most effective, have curved blades with concave cutting edges. They vary from 25cm (10in) to 60cm (2ft) in length and have handles like knife handles.

Lopping shears are an extended form of pruning shears, designed to facilitate tree pruning at longer range. When pruning upper branches, it will still be necessary to use the ladder. Tree pruners, which can be up to 3.7m (12ft) in length, enable the user to do much of the work from ground level, but they require some practise before the technique can be mastered. When using the ladder, make sure that it is squarely and securely positioned. If you are working among large branches, do not try to push aside those that seem to be in the way – the spring in the branch of a tree can push you and the ladder over. Be sure that you know where branches are going to fall, and be especially careful if there are children around.

Keep your pruning equipment clean and well-oiled. Have saws regularly sharpened and lightly oil them to prevent rust.

Insects and insecticides

IDENTIFYING TROUBLES

Recognising the enemy is half the battle when attempting to defeat it. Most pests are large enough to see easily, except red spider mite. However, this can be seen clearly with a hand-lens, on the underside of leaves. Capsid bugs, although large, are seldom seen because they move quickly. The damage is obvious but by then it is too late. The common fungus diseases also have a characteristic appearance.

Some weeds have highly decorative flowers, e.g. bindweed, speedwell and oxalis, but rapidly become too much of a good thing.

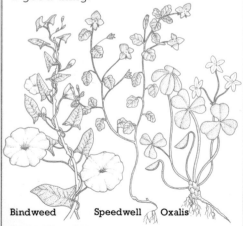

Bindweed   **Speedwell**   **Oxalis**

All insecticides are chemical; some are safe to use as far as adults, children and pets are concerned, others are harmful to some degree and precautions have to be taken. Many will damage pollinating insects or those which are parasitic to pests of garden plants.

Although there appears to be a vast and bewildering collection of garden insecticides, many of them are simply the same chemical with a different proprietary name. There is no need to keep a great stock of them in the garden shed; there are various ways of preventing trouble occurring at all, and finger-and-thumb will do a great deal to limit infestation. Moreover, it is fruit and vegetables that run into the most troubles.

But epidemics do occur in some years, especially when the right set of weather conditions coincide, and it is useful to have a weapon to hand which may just save a crop or that prize rose, which even predators cannot do in such circumstances, however hard they work.

Some of the safest, most effective and least persistent are derris, pyrethrum, malathion, and bioresmethrin, a new one analogous to pyrethrum. Soft soap or quassia solution are also safe, but less effective.

For persistent or difficult pests (leafminer, capsid bugs or red spider mite) and bad infestations, dimethoate is good. However, it is one of the heavy guns, with a blanket effect; not much will survive in the insect world, including the beneficial and pollinating insects. Fenitrothion is in the same class; it is used for caterpillar control.

For soil pests, such as cut-worm caterpillars, wireworms, leatherjackets or root-fly maggots, diazinon, a phosphorus-containing chemical, is useful, non-tainting and long-lasting. Bromophos is another alternative, phosphorus containing, but is only partially successful against cabbage root-fly.

For slugs and snails, methiocarb pellets are effective, but must be put down so that pets, children and birds cannot get at them. Many gardeners are reluctant to use systemic and tainting chemicals to kill pests, and no-one should feel obliged to use them, but it is worth bearing in mind that a short, sharp attack with something deadly may clear up the trouble for the rest of the season.

SOME COMMON PESTICIDES

PESTICIDE	USE	NOTES
Bioresmethrin	Kills aphids, thrips and other insects	New chemical, similar to pyrethrum
Bromophos	Cutworms, wireworms root flies and soil pests	In granular form only, persistent
Carbaryl	Caterpillars, weevils, earwigs, scale insects etc.	Dust or powder form; kills bees
Derris	Aphids, caterpillars, flea beetles, etc.	Dust or spray; safe and non-persistent
Diazinon	Aphids, capsids, leaf miners, red spider	Spray; persistent
Dimethoate	Aphids, red spider, leaf miner	Systemic; kills bees and fish
Gamma – HCH (Lindane)	Controls many soil, stem and leaf insects	Spray or dust; persistent – taints crops
Malathion	Aphids, whiteflies, leaf hoppers, mealy bugs etc.	Spray or dust; safe and non-persistent
Pyrethrum	Aphids, whiteflies, caterpillars	Spray; fairly safe and non-persistent
Trichlorphon	Caterpillars, leaf miners and earwigs	Spray; harmful to fish

Fungus diseases

Fungus diseases are more difficult to deal with than insect pests. There are no predators of practical use and, in the enclosed conditions of the greenhouse, they can spread extremely quickly and cause great damage.

The most useful fungicide at present is benomyl, a systemic, absorbed into the plant's sap. It destroys grey mould (*Botrytis cinerea*) and powdery mildew. However, it also kills earthworms, so moderate use is important.

Powdery mildews can also be treated with dinocap or sulphur, both of which are mainly protective, but downy mildew needs one of the so-called organic fungicides such as zineb (zinc dithiocarbamate) to deal with it. Included in this group are maneb (manganese dithiocarbamate) and thiram, both have rather specific use against various fungus diseases.

Fungicides containing sulphur or copper are the older ones, e.g. lime-sulphur, Bordeaux mixture (copper sulphate and lime), or Cheshunt compound (copper sulphate and ammonium carbonate). Some fungal diseases may easily be mistaken for virus diseases; learn to recognise them or you may destroy curable plants.

COMMON FUNGICIDES

FUNGICIDE	DISEASES	NOTES
Benomyl	Black spot, leaf mould, apple and pear scab	Systemic; apply often
Calomel	Root flies, club root, white rot	Mercurous chloride; poisonous
Dazomet	Club root and other soil-borne diseases	Persistent; irritates eyes and skin
Dinocap	Powdery mildew	Spray or powder, harmful to fish
Dichofluanid	Grey mould, downy mildew, black spot	Wettable powder; kills fish
Lime sulphur	Apple and pear scab, cane spot leaf curl	Spray; may cause leaf scorching
Maneb	Downy mildew, black spot, blight tulip fire	Spray; safe but taints crops
Quintozene	Damping off, foot rot, bulb diseases	Dust; apply to the soil
Thiophanate-methyl	Black spot, leaf mould, cane spot etc.	Systemic; needs frequent application
Thiram	Grey mould, downy mildew, leaf spot etc.	Zinc oxide powder; harmful to eyes

Bacterial diseases

Bacterial diseases are spread mainly in water, and cause much trouble on crops in store. Fleshy plant parts are most prone to infection and damage, e.g. rhubarb crown rot, soft rot of turnips or iris rhizome rot. Such diseases are often foul-smelling and reduce the plant tissue to a liquid.

Virus diseases infect the nucleus of the plant cell, and no chemical is available which will kill them, but not the plant as well.

Infected plants become stunted, grow slowly or not at all, their leaves irregularly blotched and spotted yellow, cream or other colours, they have grossly distorted or curled leaves or flowers, and streaked flower colour. Fruit ceases to appear.

Viruses are mostly carried by greenfly and other sucking insect pests, being spread as they feed. Infected plants should be completely uprooted and destroyed as soon as seen. Mosaic viruses are among the most common: they produce a yellow mottling on the leaves which then become distorted. Eventually the stricken plant collapses, but by this time many of its neighbours will be infected. Early diagnosis, therefore, is essential.

VIRUS DISEASES

◄ **Stunted growth**
Plants infected with virus diseases will not make the normal amount of growth. They will be blotched and may have curled leaves or flowers.

◄ **Blotched or spotted foliage**
Infected plants will usually show yellow, cream or greyish spots or blotches on the leaves.

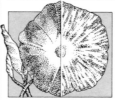

◄ **Flower and fruit damage**
The flowers of infected plants may be curled and streaked. Fruit will cease to appear.

◄ **Destroy infected plants**
Viruses cannot be cured and infected plants must be destroyed. Burn the affected plants.

Weeds and weedkillers

Weeds are usually native plants and so will grow strongly and spread easily and rapidly. Some rely on seed for their increase – the annuals and biennials such as shepherd's purse or dock. Some of these are ephemerals (chickweed), i.e. they are short-lived, needing only a few weeks from germination to flowering and setting seed. Several generations thus appear in one season. Some seed remains dormant in the soil for eight or more years.

Other weeds rely mainly on vegetative methods of increase; these are the perennials, and they spread by creeping roots or stems, or bulbils, as well as seed, e.g. creeping buttercup, couchgrass or oxalis.

Destroying the flowers of all weeds before they set seed saves a great deal of trouble; the saying 'one year's seed, seven years' weed' has been scientifically proved correct.

Small and annual weeds, growing amongst cultivated plants, can be killed with a mixture of paraquat and diquat. The same group, together with perennials, can be killed with glyphosate, though the latter will need to be treated two or three times, as new growth appears.

COMMON WEEDKILLERS

HERBICIDE	PURPOSE	NOTES
Dalapon	Clearing grass weeds	Persistent; apply in winter
Dichlobenil	Annual and perennial weeds	Persistent; harmful to trees and shrubs
Diquat	Clearing paths and borders	Effective above soil only
Ioxynil	Lawn weeds	Use on young weeds only
Mecoprop	Lawn weeds	Also checks growth of grass
Mercurous chloride	Lawn weeds	Gives short-term control
Morphamquat	Lawn weeds	Selective weedkiller that checks growth of grass
Paraquat	Total herbicide	Kills on contact; inactivated by contact with soil
Propachlor	General weed clearance	Persistent; useful in vegetable plots
Simazine	General weed clearance	Selective weedkiller; persistent
Sodium chlorate	Weed clearance in unplanted areas	Extremely persistent; best for sandy soils

Both are sprayed on to the top growth, and both are inactivated in the soil.

Where ground has to be kept clear, such as paths or drives, sodium chlorate can be watered on at varying strengths to keep them weed-free for about six months.

Alternatively, simazine can be watered on to ground free of weeds, to keep it clear for 12 months. Both these are absorbed through the roots of plants, and do not have any lasting effect on the top growth. Simazine stays where it is put; sodium chlorate will 'creep' a little in the soil.

The hormone group of weedkillers, 2·4-D, 2·4·5-T, and M.C.P.A. are sprayed on to the top growth and absorbed into the plant's sap. They damage the growing tips so badly that the plant ceases to grow and eventually dies. These weedkillers are exceedingly potent and it is difficult not to damage cultivated plants, usually as a result of drifting spray.

As with the pests and diseases, there are various methods of cultural control which will largely obviate the need for chemicals.

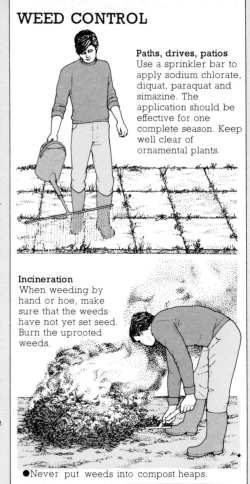

WEED CONTROL

Paths, drives, patios
Use a sprinkler bar to apply sodium chlorate, diquat, paraquat and simazine. The application should be effective for one complete season. Keep well clear of ornamental plants.

Incineration
When weeding by hand or hoe, make sure that the weeds have not yet set seed. Burn the uprooted weeds.

●Never put weeds into compost heaps.

Prevention and cure

Strong, vigorously growing plants will be much less badly affected by pests or diseases, so make sure they always have the food and moisture they require. Improve the warmth and light conditions as far as possible.

Handle plants very carefully when young, take great care not to damage their roots when transplanting, and plant so that they are upright and the roots well spread out. Be especially careful to water them adequately.

Grow disease-resistant varieties whenever available; plant at times which avoid the main life-cycle periods of insect pests. Space the plants out well, so as to avoid overcrowding.

Try companion-growing; garlic planted beneath peaches is said to prevent infection by peach leaf curl; savory grown close to broad beans wards off blackfly infestations.

Mulch round plants, to prevent weed growth.

Damp down greenhouse interiors to prevent the hot, dry atmosphere that red spider mite – and some other pests – thrive in.

Keep the garden clear of rubbish including heaps of pots, boxes, wire-netting, posts, stones and corrugated iron, and burn bonfire material frequently. Do not put badly diseased or pest-ridden plants on to the compost heap, nor the most persistent weeds, such as oxalis, horsetail, couch-grass and so on. Remove dead or dying herbaceous plants, branches, shrubs or trees and destroy them.

Finally, remember that it is claimed that plants grown organically, that is, completely without artificial fertilizers or pesticides, do not suffer from pest or disease infections.

Observation

The most important part of treatment is observation. If you get into the habit of going round your plants more or less every day, you will unconsciously be assessing their state of growth and health. Anything out of the ordinary will be seen almost as soon as it appears, including pests and diseases, or their effects.

If a casual glance reveals one green-fly, an intensive search will turn up another 20 lurking under a leaf or two. A quick bit of finger and thumb work will dispose of that group before it turns into 50 the next day.

Hand removal of many other pests will do a great deal to keep plants clean.

The introduction of predatory insects obviates the need for chemicals. Whitefly and red spider mite can both be destroyed in this way, and supplies can be obtained by companies specialising in this method of control. A bacterial solution for spraying on to cabbage caterpillars is also commercially available.

The naturally occurring beneficial insects include ladybirds, the adults and larvae of which both need greenfly in their diet. Care in choice of chemical spray will ensure that as many of these as possible are spared.

Slugs and snails can be trapped with containers of diluted beer or sugary milk sunk in the ground. Soil pests can be attracted to baits of potato or carrot skewered and buried in the soil, and then removed daily, to kill the catch manually.

Some chemicals are specific to a pest, and do not harm anything else. Application in the evening, and avoidance of flowers when spraying minimises damage to pollinating insects.

Use the stronger chemicals only as a last resort, but then use them thoroughly, so that they need not be used again that season.

For best and safest effects of all these materials, use them exactly as the manufacturers direct, particularly with regard to precautions, and the interval of time between spraying and harvesting edible crops.

Spray or dust in calm weather, make sure plants are growing in moist soil or compost, and treat the underside of leaves, as this is where many pests live and feed.

Wash apparatus thoroughly afterwards, and throw away excess solution, as it breaks down chemically, preferably into drains or unused patches of soil. Keep all out of reach of children and pets, and make sure all are clearly labelled all the time.

Controlling blackfly
Blackfly can be killed with any of the pesticides which control aphids. They can be stopped by less drastic methods however; removing them with finger and thumb being the best method.

89

Glossary of terms

Annual
A plant which will complete its cycle from germination to setting seed within one year. Hardy annuals may be sown out-of-doors in spring, or in August/September for early flowering the following year. Half-hardy annuals must be raised under glass in early spring, or sown out-of-doors when all danger of frost has passed.

Biennial
A plant which takes two years to complete the cycle from germination to setting of seed.

Cordon
A method of training fruit trees so that all side growth can be pruned very close to the main stem or stems. Main stems are very often trained diagonally against wires or supports.

Drill
A shallow groove, usually from $\frac{1}{2}$in (12.5mm) to 4ins (10cm) deep, made in the soil with a hoe or rake – into which seeds will be sown.

Espalier
A method of training fruit trees so that they may be grown against fences or walls. The main stem remains vertical, but branches are trained at right angles along wires.

Germination
The emergence of the first growing shoots from a seed.

Hardening-off
The gradual introduction of plants to outdoor conditions. This may take the form of a cold frame for plants raised in heated greenhouses, or the opening of a frame for gradually increasing periods.

Herbaceous
Any plant having soft growth – as opposed to woody.

Perennial
A plant which continually repeats the flowering-seeding cycle. The cycle need not occur every year – in fact, it need not occur at all; a plant which lives for many years without flowering is also a perennial.

Photosynthesis
The process by which plants convert solar energy into the foods that they need for growth and development.

Plumule
The first growing shoot of a plant. It develops to become the main stem.

Potash
The common name for Potassium carbonate, the principle fruit forming fertilizer.

Propagation
The general term for plant increase, whether by seed, cuttings, layering, budding, grafting – or any other method.

Radicle
At germination, the radicle emerges at the same time as the plumule and becomes the principle root stem. A network of fibrous roots begins to develop after a few days.

Shrub
Any plant which has a tough woody growth, and is not a tree, is a shrub. Shrubs may be deciduous or evergreen, coniferous or broad-leaved.

Spit
The term used for the digging part of a spade. In other words, digging one spit deep means digging to the full depth of the spade.

Tilth
The word used to describe a fine, soft, crumbly soil texture – ideal for sowing and planting. Derived from the word 'till'.

Tine
The term used for the prongs of a garden fork – corresponds to spit.

Index

93

Index

▶Use the chart on page 95 to enter the dates of sowings, plantings etc., so that you can keep a log of the progress of the crops in your garden.

Keep your own records

VEGETABLE	SOW/PLANT – DATES	HARVEST – DATES	NOTES

Acknowledgments

The 'How To' Book of
Basic Gardening was created
by Simon Jennings and Company
Limited. We are grateful to
the following individuals and
organisations for their
assistance in the making of
this book:

Arthur Baker: *line illustrations*
Nigel Chamberlain: *line illustrations*
John Couzins: *cover and title page photographs*
The Dover Archive: *engravings and embellishments*
Carole Johnson: *line illustrations*
Richard Lewis: *line illustrations*
Coral Mula: *line illustrations*
Robert Micklewright: *line illustrations*
Christopher Perry: *additional artwork*
Anna Pavord: *compilation of index*
Ransome, Simms and Jefferies Ltd., Ipswich: *engraving
of the first lawnmower*
Southwood's Garden Centre: *for the loan of gardening
equipment*
St. Petersberg Press: *painting by David Hockney, p23*
Michael Woods: *line illustrations*
Yale Centre for British Art: *painting pages 6/7*
Helena Zakrsewska – Rucinska: *hand tinting of engravings*

Photographs:
Pat Brindley: pages 11 *t, bl, br*; 14 *t, b*; 15 *t, bl*;
18 *tl, bl, br*; 22 *b*; 23 *br, br*; 27 *b*; 30 *t, b*;
31 *t, bl, br*
Tom Buckeridge: pages 10; 15 *br*; 30

abbreviations: *t* top; *b* bottom; *c* centre; *tl* top left; *tr* top right;
bl bottom left; *br* bottom right; *r* right

Typesetting by Servis Filmsetting Ltd., Manchester
Headline setting by Facet Photosetting, London

Special thanks to Norman Ruffell and
the staff of Swaingrove Ltd., Bury St. Edmunds,
Suffolk, for the lithographic reproduction.

'HOW TO'